Bring the Goddess into Your Kitchen

We all have a trace of the Goddess within us.

Recipes from a Vegetarian Goddess is a sensual journey through vegetarian foods and Goddess festivals, peppered with bits of information on different Goddesses and their roles in the changing seasons. It's the perfect cookbook for anyone who is interested in expanding his/her repertoire to include meatless meals—without giving up an ounce of pleasure or flavor.

My recipe offerings are uncomplicated and easy to prepare: try my fettuccini with asparagus and lemon (a lovely spring pasta tossed in a light lemony sauce) or fire up the grill and make marinated grilled vegetables in balsamic vinegar and fresh garlic. There's also penne Mediterraneo, a delicious pasta seductively infused with the Mediterranean flavors of garlic, lemon, fresh mint, and tossed with toasted pine nuts. Or try grilled polenta topped with a colorful assortment of roasted vegetables and melting creamy goat cheese.

I include everything you need to make a memorable vegetarian meal, from tempting appetizers and breads, to pizzas, calzones, and easy risottos, even picnic foods. Desserts include apple cake, homemade coconut ice cream with chocolate chips, and old-fashioned, baked pear crisp with cinnamon and brown sugar.

May you find inspiration here to celebrate the Goddess and her seasons by creating fresh, healthy meals for yourself and those you love.

Thank you,

About the Author

A graduate of the Corcoran School of Art, Washington, DC, Karri Allrich has been working as a professional artist for over twenty years, exhibiting her award-winning paintings in one-woman gallery shows and juried exhibitions. Karri's work has been reproduced by fine art card companies and published as limited edition prints.

As she compiled over twenty years of her vegetarian recipes for this cookbook, Karri began to integrate other aspects of her life into the project, exploring her love of nature, living in tune with the four seasons, honoring her intuition, and getting in touch with aspects of the feminine Goddess. Karri resides in Massachusetts with her husband and two children.

To Write to the Author

If you wish to contact the author or would like more information about this book, please write to the author in care of Llewellyn Worldwide and we will forward your request. Both the author and publisher appreciate hearing from you and learning of your enjoyment of this book and how it has helped you. Llewellyn Worldwide cannot guarantee that every letter written to the author can be answered, but all will be forwarded. Please write to:

Karri Allrich
℅ Llewellyn Worldwide
P.O. Box 64383, Dept. K016-7
St. Paul, MN 55164-0383, U.S.A.

Please enclose a self-addressed, stamped envelope for reply, or $1.00 to cover costs.
If outside U.S.A., enclose international postal reply coupon.

Recipes from a
Vegetarian Goddess

Delectable
Feasts
Through
the Seasons

Karri Allrich

2000
Llewellyn Publications
St. Paul, Minnesota 55164-0383, U.S.A.

FIRST EDITION
First printing, 2000

Cover art: Karri Allrich
Cover design: Anne Marie Garrison
Editing and book design: Christine Snow
Illustrations: Shelly Bartek

Library of Congress Cataloging-in-Publication Data

Allrich, Karri.
   Recipes from a vegetarian goddess: delectable feasts through the seasons / Karri Allrich — 1st ed.
      p. cm.
   Includes index.
   ISBN 1-56718-016-7
   1. Vegetarian cookery. I. Title.
   TX837.A383 2000
   641.5'636—dc21   99-462300

Llewellyn Worldwide does not participate in, endorse, or have any authority or responsibility concerning private business transactions between our authors and the public.

All mail addressed to the author is forwarded but the publisher cannot, unless specifically instructed by the author, give out an address or phone number.

Llewellyn Publications
A Division of Llewellyn Worldwide, Ltd.
P.O. Box 64383, Dept. K016-7
St. Paul, MN 55164-0383
www.llewellyn.com

Printed on recycled paper in the United States of America

Acknowledgments

I would like to express my passionate appreciation to those who so agreeably volunteered to taste-test my recipes over the course of writing this book: Dorothy and Alan; Lori and Gilles; Lynn and John; Marty and Stan; Katya; Nancy; Kristen and Tim; and Alex, Colin, and Steve.

Abundant thanks to the Kitchen Goddesses who helped test recipes in their own domain: Nancy Brezin, Dorothy Somerville, and Lynn Cart.

A bounty of appreciation to all of the Goddesses in my life: Martha, my soul sister; Katya, my dream sister; Lori, my feline loving sister; Helen, my art rep extraordinaire; Del and Harriet, my support and inspiration; and the women of my Dream Circle.

Thanks also to those at Llewellyn who believed in my project: Nancy Mostad, Ann Kerns, Christine Snow, Lynne Menturweck, and Anne Marie Garrison.

And finally, my deepest gratitude to the Great Goddess in her myriad guises, whose generous gifts enrich my life. . . .

Brightest Blessings.

For my husband Steve

who seems to take pleasure in everything I do.

I have blossomed under this gift.

And to our sons, Colin and Alex,

whom I have taken such pleasure in . . .

from the very start.

Contents

Introduction

Feasts and the Goddess

By aligning ourselves to Nature's cycles, we bring the Goddess back into our everyday awareness. One way to enhance our awareness is through food and celebration. This connection between food, feast, and the Goddess is an ancient one. Earliest peoples worshipped Mother Earth, Gaia, as the Great Provider, finding sustenance in her seeds, roots, and fruit and healing in her herbs and sparkling waters. Within her caves and caverns they found shelter.

As agriculture flourished, so did gratitude of the Great Mother's fertility. The Wheel of the Year was marked and celebrated by the turning of the seasons, reflecting the close tie to the earth's cycle of planting, growth, harvest, and dormancy. Stories and myths emerged to symbolize this ongoing dance between the Goddess, earth, and her Consort, the sun.

Seeking the Goddess Today

In seeking the nature of the Goddess today, we are searching for a path that turns in harmony with the earth, Our Mother, in tune with her seasons and changes. To grow in understanding of the elegance within her wisdom is to learn to surrender to her mystery. The Goddess as Great Mother, Gaia, has much to teach us, if we only take the time to listen to her lessons, to celebrate her offerings, to respect her natural balance.

Incorporating the rhythm of the seasons' changes into our daily awareness of foods, nourishment, and pleasure helps us to honor the Goddess and celebrate her many gifts. Through feasts and holidays we learn about our own selves reflected in her symbolic stories and her many guises. We revel in her complexity of nourishment, the wisdom in her seasonal offerings.

In *Recipes from a Vegetarian Goddess,* we follow the Wheel of the Year, with recipes designed to celebrate what each season bestows, including menus for special feasts, such as Imbolc or Summer Solstice, and notes about the Goddess in her myriad guises, from Brigid to Hecate.

Calling Upon the Goddess

We all have a trace of the Goddess in us. We call upon Hestia, keeper of the hearth, as we patiently stir a soul-satisfying soup. Aphrodite whispers in our ear as we select fresh-cut flowers for the table, light candles, and set out chilled wine glasses. Even Artemis had to eat. She calls to us to pack up a picnic basket and join her spirit in the wild beauty of nature, urging us to pause at the music of a rushing stream, to marvel at the rising moon, and drink in the wash of emerging stars.

Food As Connection

This cookbook project has evolved from my own desire to integrate the various aspects of the Goddess in my own life. Being an artist, wife, mother, daughter, sister, and friend, the one thread through all of these different roles is food.

Food, and the pleasure it brings when sharing it with those I love, has been my connecting cord. Such a simple idea that this daily practice of finding nourishment and sharing sustenance is also a means of connection, a way to nurture body and soul; a way to celebrate the presence of the Goddess.

In this challenging era of frantic activity, instant meals, and obsessive dieting, the Goddess is calling to us: "Slow down!" she urges, "Celebrate my bounty." Let us then rekindle our joy of food and take pleasure in creating fresh, nourishing feasts to share at our table.

Notes on Being (Mostly) Vegetarian

I have been mostly vegetarian for thirty years now, thriving on the challenge of creating meals without meat. The beauty of cooking vegetarian is that it opens up a world of possibilities, expanding our awareness of other cultures and cuisine beyond the limits of our inheritance. In discovering new world flavors, I aroused my senses with spices and herbs and experimented with the fruity taste of extra virgin olive oil, the creamy texture of risotto and earthy polenta, the fire of red chiles, and the heady fragrance of breads baked with fresh rosemary. The litany of brown rice and steamed vegetables that once dominated vegetarian cuisine paled against the flavor and variety I found in world cuisine. And so I began my journey, creating vegetarian recipes that enlivened my senses and celebrated the Goddess with pleasure and flavor.

Simple Pleasures

Today the Goddess gently urges us to make time for the simple pleasures in life; to enjoy her seasons, her abundance. From the dark distinctive taste of an early morning mug of coffee, to inhaling the intoxicating aroma of some fresh garlic rubbed on a slice of warm crusty bread, she welcomes us to the simple sensual pleasures. So breathe deeply during a quiet, solitary walk. Run your fingers over the softness of fresh herbs growing in the garden, inhaling their magickal fragrance. Lie back on the sweet grass and watch the shifting clouds above. Make note of the moon and watch her waxing and waning, bathing in her silver light.

Inspiration

My simple wish in offering you this book is that you delight in discovering some new flavors and possibilities inside these pages, whether you are a part-time Vegetarian Goddess, a full-time Vegetarian Goddess, or simply a Goddess who is looking for some new and creative ways to include more diverse foods into your weekly menu or holiday festivities.

May you find inspiration here to create more pleasure in your life, to celebrate the Goddess, to explore new flavor combinations, and enjoy the culinary art of creating and sharing fresh healthy meals with those you love.

A Vegetarian Goddess' Pantry

Here is a list of must-have-on-hand items that make any Goddess' menu planning easier. Be sure to choose wholesome, organic foods whenever possible. What's good for the planet is good for us all.

Almond milk

Apples

Apple juice

Artichokes, canned or frozen

Baking powder

Baking soda

Beans, canned: black beans, black-eyed peas, chili beans, chickpeas, kidney, pinto, white northern (cannellini)

Black olives

Bread crumbs, Italian style

Canola oil

Caraway seeds

Cheeses: Asiago, goat cheese, Gruyère, feta, Parmesan, Romano, soy

Chili sauce

Cocoa

Coconut milk, light

Cornmeal, stone-ground

Couscous

Cranberries, dried

Currants

Dijon mustard

Flour, unbleached all-purpose

Frozen veggies: corn, peas

Garlic

Granola, light

Green chiles, canned

Green olives

Herbs: basil, bay leaf, chives, cilantro, dill, Italian herbs, oregano, parsley, marjoram, mint, rosemary, thyme

Honey

Lemons

Lentils

Limes

Maple syrup

Molasses

Nuts: almonds, hazelnuts, peanuts, pecans, pine nuts, walnuts

Oats

Olive oil, extra-virgin
Onions: red, sweet yellow
Pasta: angel hair, farfalle, fettuccine, lasagna, linguini, penne, rigatoni, spaghetti, tortellini, ziti
Peanut butter, natural
Peanut oil
Peppercorns
Polenta, quick-cooking
Potatoes: new, red, yellow, sweet
Raisins
Rice: arborio, basmati, brown, pilaf, Texmati, wild
Salsa
Sea salt
Sesame oil
Sesame seeds
Sherry, dry
Soy sauce

Spices: cinnamon, cloves, chili powder, chili flakes, Chinese five-spice powder, cumin, curry powder, ginger root, nutmeg
Split peas
Sugar: brown, natural, white
Tofu: silken, firm
Tomatoes, canned: whole, diced
Tomato sauce, good jarred pasta sauce
Tortillas: corn, flour
Vanilla extract: bourbon or Mexican
Vegetable bouillon, cubes
Vegetable broth
Vinegar: balsamic, cider, raspberry, rice, sherry, wine
Wine for cooking: red, white
Xanthan gum (to give ice cream a smooth texture)
Yeast, bread

Vegetarian Goddess Recipes

In spring, we encounter the Goddess in her maiden aspect, full of life and **promise**. At the vernal equinox, when day and night are in balance, she is the Goddess Ostara, **youth** and fertility incarnate—**life** awakening unto itself. By May 1 she is Maid Marion, bedecked with **flowers**, dancing merrily about a May Pole, hoping to catch a glimpse of Robin Hood, the Green Man of the forest.

Spring finds the Goddess standing in the east. It is **sunrise**, and her maiden dress is yellow. Her element is air, and she breathes in **joy** and inspiration. This is a **heady** time, a time of new growth and lengthening daylight, a time for fresh new foods and **cleansing** herbs. It is a time to **renew** ourselves and get back in touch with the awakening earth.

Spring

Festival Menus

Spring Equinox (aka Ostara)

It is the time of rebirth, the spring equinox, when the dark (feminine) is in balance with the light (masculine). We celebrate Ostara, a fire festival in honor of the Goddess of the Dawn. We color eggs in honor of her fertility. Chocolate rabbits remind us of mating rituals and the creation of new life. Dogwoods are in bloom. Gather iris and narcissus for your table. Light green candles for growth and prosperity, and pink for love. The warmer days are upon us and we are revitalized as the great Goddess Isis, Mother Moon, blows her cleansing winds across the earth.

Curried Stuffed Eggs *(page 8)*

Cilantro Pesto *(page 9)*

Cream of Carrot Soup *(page 18)*

Fettuccine with Asparagus and Lemon *(page 29)*

Golden Carrot Cake *(page 43)*

May Day (aka Beltane)

It is the start of the summer season . . . let the festivities begin! May Day is a day for flowers and music, dancing and feasting. Aphrodite, the Goddess of love and passion, beauty, and art is in her glory. Flora, the Roman Goddess of blossoms and gardens, honors all growing things and celebrates pleasure. Beltane is a fire festival, reveling in fertility and sensuality.

The colorful dance around the May Pole symbolizes the weaving of feminine and masculine energies, with joy and abandon. Let yourself go with the flow today, feast with your loved ones, and bask in the beauty of the season.

May Wine *(page 7)*

Roasted Garlic *(page 10)*

Peanut Soup *(page 17)*

Lemon Risotto with Baby Peas *(page 30)*

Tomatoes in Creamy Lime and Chili Dressing *(page 40)*

Chocolate-Almond Coconut Ice Cream *(page 42)*

Beverages and Bites

May Wine

What would a celebration of May Day be without some proper libation? Try this charming combination of white wine and strawberries.

1   bottle strawberry or
    cherry juice
1   bottle white wine,
    chilled, such as
    chardonnay
1   bottle strawberry or
    pear juice, chilled
1   pint ripe strawberries,
    stemmed, washed,
    sliced
    Sweet woodruff
    (optional)

Using one bottle of strawberry or cherry juice, make "ice cubes" the night before. On the day of your feast, combine the chilled white wine with the chilled juice in a large container. Wrap the sweet woodruff in a piece of cheesecloth to make an infusion, and immerse the herb into the beverage. Keep chilled for one hour.

Remove the bag, pour the wine mixture into a serving bowl or pitcher, and add in the sliced strawberries and juice ice cubes. Have a toast to Isis, the Great Goddess, our Protector.

Note: Sweet woodruff is an old-fashioned Victorian herb traditionally used to make May Wine. It may not be readily available in most stores, so that's why it is optional.

Curried Stuffed Eggs

Serving these savory eggs at the spring equinox has become a family tradition for us. What an appropriate symbol is the humble egg, celebrating our earth's yearly rebirth and honoring life's very potential.

6	free-range eggs, hard-boiled, cooled
1–3	tablespoons soy mayonnaise or egg mayonnaise
	Sherry or red wine vinegar
1½	teaspoons Dijon mustard
2	teaspoons minced red onion
2	teaspoons finely chopped jalapeños or green chiles
1	teaspoon curry powder
	Sea salt
	White pepper, freshly ground
	Sweet paprika
	Fresh chives or cilantro, chopped

Carefully slice the cooled eggs in half, lengthwise. Gently scoop out the yolks into a small mixing bowl. Mash the yolks with a fork and add enough mayonnaise to moisten. Add the vinegar and mustard, blending well. Add the onion, jalapeños, and curry, mixing together until smooth and creamy. Taste for seasoning adjustments, adding salt and white pepper, if desired.

Spoon the filling into each egg half and place the eggs on a serving platter. Dust lightly with paprika and some chopped fresh chives or cilantro.

Serves 4–6.

Cilantro Pesto

Here is a change from the usual basil pesto. The fresh, lively taste of cilantro lends itself beautifully to any appetizer, perking up your taste after a long winter. Serve it on crostini or bruschetta, add it to soups, or spread it on pizza.

3	cups fresh cilantro, firmly packed
6	garlic cloves, peeled
¼	cup pine nuts
3	tablespoons extra-virgin olive oil
1	tablespoon lime juice
1	tablespoon balsamic vinegar
⅛	teaspoon chili flakes
	Sea salt

Combine all of the ingredients in a food processor or blender and purée until it becomes a smooth paste. Cover and chill for 2 hours. Serve this pesto as an appetizer spread with *Crostini* (Winter, page 154).

Serving ideas

- Toss it with hot, moist pasta.
- Spoon it on pizza dough for a Southwestern-style pizza, topped with roasted vegetables and jack cheese.

Roasted Garlic

Add the element of fire to your Beltane feast with soft fragrant heads of roasted garlic, ready for your guests to spread on toasted bread or vegetables . . . whatever they desire!

4–6 heads of garlic
4 tablespoons extra-virgin olive oil

Preheat oven to 350 degrees (or fire up the grill to medium heat). Take the heads of garlic and remove as much of the loose papery skin that you can without causing the outer cloves to fall off. Slice across the top of the head to expose the upper cloves. Carefully slice the tips off of the side cloves to expose them as well.

Place the garlic heads on a square of aluminum foil and drizzle with the olive oil, moistening all of the exposed cloves. Fold and seal the foil and bake for about 50–60 minutes. The aroma will be intoxicating! (On an outdoor grill, it roasts faster, so place it on a higher rack and keep an eye on it, checking after 15–20 minutes.)

Garlic is done when the cloves are soft and can be squeezed easily out of their skins. Roasted garlic can be used in recipes in place of fresh garlic for a more mellow flavor.

Serving ideas

- Use roasted garlic as an appetizer paste on *Crostini* (Winter, page 154).
- Place the whole roasted heads of garlic at the center of an antipasti plate, where cloves can be plucked for eating alongside olives, pepperoncini, cheeses, marinated artichokes, and other antipasti.

Bruschetta

An Italian favorite, make this light and flavorful offering in honor of Venus, Moon Goddess of the Romans, the quintessential lover. And see what happens! You can prepare bruschetta as an appetizer using a baguette, or make a supper out of it by slicing up a large crusty peasant loaf and adding crisp spring greens accented with ripe olives.

1	baguette or 4 hearty slices from a peasant-style loaf
3–4	garlic cloves, peeled, sliced in half
6	ripe roma tomatoes, chopped
6	garlic cloves, minced
1	cup fresh chopped basil
½	tablespoon marjoram
	Sea salt
	Black pepper, freshly ground
4	tablespoons extra-virgin olive oil
½	cup crumbled feta cheese
	Baby salad greens (optional)
5–7	kalamata olives (optional)

Preheat oven to 450 degrees. Slice the bread on a slight diagonal and lay on a cookie sheet. Toast the bread lightly in a hot oven, for a few minutes only. Remove and rub the hot bread with fresh cut garlic. Set aside.

In a medium bowl, combine the tomatoes, minced garlic, basil, marjoram, sea salt, freshly ground black pepper, and olive oil. Let sit for 15 minutes.

On individual salad plates, place a slice of the toasted garlic bread. Divide the tomato mixture among the slices and top with crumbled feta cheese. Add a sampling of baby greens around the bread and drizzle with extra-virgin olive oil and kalamata olives.

Serves 4.

Serving idea

- To serve as an appetizer, use a French baguette to make *Crostini* (see Winter, page 154). Serve the tomato mixture in an attractive bowl at the center of a large platter or rustic bread board, surrounded by the crostini, and offer spoons and plenty of napkins.

Sun-Dried Tomato Focaccia

My favorite Italian bread, the tender focaccia, makes a wonderful picnic bread. Artemis and Aphrodite beckon . . . on the first warm and spring-like afternoon of the season, pack this flavorful loaf, take a container of mixed olives, a bottle of good chianti, and a blanket, and invite your love to come celebrate spring. (Don't forget the wine glasses.)

1½	teaspoons dry active yeast
1¼	cups warm water
3	cups unbleached flour
1	tablespoon cornmeal
1	teaspoon sea salt
1	tablespoon honey
3	tablespoons extra-virgin olive oil
15	sun-dried tomatoes (dry-packed), soaked in hot water till moist, drained, chopped
5	garlic cloves, minced
1	tablespoon Italian herbs
1	teaspoon chili flakes
1–2	tablespoons extra-virgin olive oil
	Coarse sea salt

Bread machine: Set the cycle for "dough" and "large loaf." Add the ingredients in the order your particular manufacturer recommends.

By hand: Combine the ingredients as you would to make a loaf of bread: dissolve yeast in warm water, and add the honey. Combine the other ingredients (from olive oil to chili flakes) in a mixing bowl, add the yeast and water, and mix well. When the dough easily forms a ball, place it on a floured board and knead for 7–10 minutes. Focaccia dough should be moist. Place dough in an oiled bowl and cover with oiled plastic wrap. Set it in a warm place to rest and let rise for 45–60 minutes.

After the dough has risen in your bread machine or bowl, turn it out onto a board dusted with cornmeal. Sprinkle the surface with cornmeal and, using a rolling pin or your hands, shape it into a 12 to 14-inch flat oval or circle. Sprinkle a baking sheet with cornmeal and move the flattened dough to the pan. Brush the top surface with olive oil, sprinkle with coarse sea salt, and cover with a clean towel. Set aside to let it rise for 20 minutes, or until doubled in height.

(If you are using a pizza stone, place the flattened dough on a peel dusted with cornmeal, brush with oil, cover, and let rise.)

continued

Preheat your oven to 400 degrees. (If using a pizza stone, warm it in the oven during the 20 minutes the focaccia is rising.)

Place the focaccia into the oven. Bake for 10 minutes in the upper half of your oven, then reduce the temperature to 350 degrees and continue to bake until the bread is golden brown, about 12–15 minutes. Remove from the oven and cool on a wire rack. Serve warm or at room temperature.

Serves 6–8.

Serving idea

- Leftover slices of focaccia are wonderful toasted and drizzled with olive oil.

Seasonal Soups

Tomato Basil Soup

To evoke the Goddess of Love, Aphrodite, entice your lover with a bowl of this light, fresh soup, crafted from the fruit of love: the tomato! Sit together at the window and watch the spring rain drench the new daffodil shoots.

2 tablespoons extra-virgin olive oil
1 onion, chopped fine
2 garlic cloves, minced
1 can (28 ounces) crushed tomatoes
1 medium potato, peeled, diced
2 cups tomato juice
2 teaspoons sugar
1 bay leaf
  Sea salt
  White pepper, freshly ground
2 cups milk or nondairy milk
¼ cup chopped fresh basil
2 tablespoons chopped fresh Italian parsley
  Nutmeg

In a heavy soup pot, heat the olive oil over medium heat and sauté the onion and garlic lightly for 4–5 minutes. Add in the canned tomatoes, potato, tomato juice, sugar, bay leaf, sea salt, and white pepper. Stir together and bring to a high simmer. Reduce heat and simmer for 20 minutes.

Slowly stir in milk, herbs, and a pinch of nutmeg. Gently heat through, without boiling. Serve piping hot with some warm cornbread or focaccia.

Serves 4.

Split Pea Soup with Mint

Perfect for those blustery March days, this Vegetarian Goddess version of a classic split pea soup is the very color of spring green, topped with fresh fragrant mint.

2   tablespoons extra-virgin olive oil
1   Vidalia onion, diced
2   celery stalks, chopped
2   carrots, peeled, chopped
4   garlic cloves, crushed
1¾ cups dried split peas
5   cups light vegetable broth
½–1 cup water, as needed
¼   cup dry vermouth, or vodka
1   bay leaf
¼   teaspoon rosemary
    Sea salt
    White pepper, freshly ground
    Light sour cream (optional)
½   cup fresh chopped mint

In a heavy soup pot, heat the olive oil over medium heat. Sauté the onion and celery for 5 minutes. Add in the garlic and stir for 1 minute. Add the split peas, vegetable broth, ½ cup water, vermouth, bay leaf, and rosemary and stir well. Bring to a boil, then reduce heat to a simmer for about 1 hour, or until peas are tender. Remove the bay leaf.

Ladle ¾ of the soup into a blender, in small batches if necessary, cover, and purée for 3–4 minutes until smooth, adding more water to thin if needed. Pour the purée back into the soup pot with the remaining split peas and stir well to blend. Gently heat through. Taste for seasoning adjustments and add salt and white pepper, if desired.

Serve in bowls with a swirl of light sour cream and garnish with fresh chopped mint.

Serves 4.

Peanut Soup

Create some earth magick with this incredibly delicious soup, stirring up masculine energy for the fires of Beltane. The heating elements of the garlic and onion increase passion . . . and warm the heart.

2 tablespoons sesame oil or peanut oil

1 onion, diced

2 stalks celery, finely chopped

5 garlic cloves, minced

4 carrots, peeled, chopped

5 cups vegetable broth

1 cup water

⅔ cup smooth natural peanut butter

3 tablespoons tomato paste

Sea salt

White pepper, freshly ground

½ cup fresh cilantro, chopped

Heat the oil in a heavy soup pot and sauté the onion for 3 minutes. Add in the celery and garlic, stir well, and sauté for 3 minutes. Add the carrots and cook for another 3 minutes. Pour in the broth and water and bring to a high simmer. Reduce heat and slowly simmer for 15–20 minutes, until the vegetables are tender.

In a large glass measuring cup, combine the peanut butter and tomato paste with a ladle full of hot broth from the soup pot. Stir together to make a paste. Slowly add this paste to the pot, stirring to blend well. Let the soup simmer slowly for about 15–20 minutes, until the peanut oil rises to the top surface. Skim this oil off with a large flat vinyl spoon. (It will take several passes to retrieve all of the oil.)

Season with sea salt and ground white pepper. Serve this creamy soup in colorful bowls with a garnish of fresh chopped cilantro.

Serves 4–6.

Cream of Carrot Soup

A smooth and inviting soup that makes a perfect beginning for celebrating the Lady of Spring, Ostara. Its beautiful creamy orange color will complement your spring table. Fill a pitcher with bright daffodils and rejoice in the season of awakenings.

2	tablespoons extra-virgin olive oil
2	medium leeks, white and light green parts only, chopped
3	cups carrots, peeled, chopped
2	teaspoons sugar
5	cups vegetable broth
⅛	cup dry sherry
1	cup plain almond milk or milk
2	tablespoons chopped fresh parsley
2	tablespoons chopped fresh dill
	Sea salt
	White pepper, freshly ground
	Nutmeg

In a heavy soup pot, heat the olive oil over medium heat and sauté the leeks for 3–4 minutes. Add the carrots and sugar and stir together. Add in the vegetable broth and sherry and bring to a boil. Cover and reduce heat. Simmer for 15 minutes or so, until the carrots are tender.

Ladle the soup into a blender, in small batches if necessary, and cover. Purée for 2–3 minutes, until smooth. Return the purée to the soup pot and stir in the milk and fresh herbs. Add sea salt, white pepper, and a pinch of nutmeg, to your taste, and heat through gently, taking care not to boil. Serve immediately.

Serves 4 as a meal, 6 as an appetizer.

Everyday Feasts

Spaghetti for a Rainy Day

Stir up some love magick in the kitchen with the fire of chiles and garlic. This is a simple, satisfying dish sure to heat up your passions on a rainy day. Toss in some fresh parsley for luck!

1	pound Italian spaghetti pasta, cooked, drained
⅔	cup extra-virgin olive oil
8–10	garlic cloves, minced
1	teaspoon red chili flakes
	Sea salt
	Black pepper, freshly ground
2–3	tablespoons chopped fresh Italian parsley

While the spaghetti is cooking to al dente in salted water, heat the olive oil gently in a large, wide nonstick skillet over low-medium heat. Stir in the garlic, chili flakes, sea salt, and ground pepper and gently warm the seasonings.

Drain the pasta and reserve about a half cup of the pasta liquid. Add the pasta and reserved water into the warm olive oil mixture, add in the chopped parsley, and toss the spaghetti well to coat it evenly.

Serve at once in pasta bowls with slices of warm crusty bread to soak up any remaining oil and garlic left in your dish . . . you won't want to waste a drop!

Serves 4–5.

Penne Rustica

The Roman Goddess Flora might have created this recipe herself. Her earthy sensuality and love for flowers and green growing things made her the embodiment of pleasure and beauty.

1 pound Italian penne pasta

2 tablespoons extra-virgin olive oil

1 red onion, sliced in chunks

1 red pepper, cored, seeded, chopped

1 yellow pepper, cored, seeded, chopped

1 package cremini mushrooms, sliced

5–6 garlic cloves, minced

2 tablespoons capers, rinsed

5–6 roma tomatoes, seeded, chopped

Sea salt

Black pepper, freshly ground

¼ teaspoon red pepper flakes

12–15 ripe olives or kalamata olives

1 bunch of fresh basil, shredded

Several sprigs of fresh marjoram, leaves stripped, or ½ tablespoon dried

3–4 ounces feta cheese, crumbled

Bring a large pot of salted water to a rolling boil and cook the penne until al dente. Heat the olive oil in a large nonstick skillet over medium heat and sauté the onion until it softens, about 5 minutes. Add in the red and yellow peppers and stir, cooking for another 5–7 minutes.

Toss in mushrooms, garlic, capers, and chopped tomatoes. Add a pinch of sea salt, freshly ground pepper, and red pepper flakes and stir. When peppers and mushrooms are soft and tender, add the olives, shredded basil, and marjoram leaves. Mix well and turn heat down to low.

When pasta is done, drain and drizzle on a little olive oil to keep it from sticking. Place the pasta in a warmed serving bowl and add the sautéed vegetables and crumbled feta cheese. Toss all of the ingredients gently and serve immediately.

A crisp salad of baby greens dressed in a *Balsamic Vinaigrette* (Winter, page 186) and a side of peasant-style bread completes this rustic feast.

Serves 4–5.

Pasta Primavera

This appetizing dish could also be called Aphrodite's Pasta. Set the mood with glowing rose-colored candles and chilled glasses of white wine. Then grab your love by the hand and step outside to drink in the colors of the sunset.

1   pound Italian linguini
1   cup frozen baby peas
3   tablespoons extra-virgin olive oil
1   cup diced Spanish onion
1   medium leek, white and light green parts only, sliced
4   garlic cloves, chopped
1   large carrot, peeled, julienned
½   cup chopped red bell pepper
1   cup green beans, cut into 2-inch lengths
1   medium zucchini, sliced, quartered
1   cup chopped roma tomatoes
1   cup vegetable broth
¼   cup dry white wine
¼   cup chopped fresh parsley
    Sea salt
    White pepper, freshly ground
3   tablespoons cream or soy cream
½   cup chopped fresh basil
½   cup shredded Parmesan or Romano cheese
    Fresh parsley, chopped

Bring a large pot of salted water to a rolling boil and cook the linguini till al dente. During the last 4–5 minutes of cooking the pasta, add the frozen baby peas.

Heat the olive oil in a large skillet over medium heat and sauté the onion and leek for 5 minutes. Add the garlic, carrot, and red pepper and sauté for 2 minutes. Add the green beans, zucchini, tomatoes, vegetable broth, wine, parsley, sea salt, and white pepper. Bring to a high simmer, then lower the heat and cook for 3–5 minutes, until the veggies are tender. Stir in the cream and fresh basil.

Drain the pasta and peas and pour into a warmed serving bowl. Add ½ cup Parmesan and mix together, then add the skillet vegetables and sauce and toss together well.

Garnish with a dusting of Parmesan and some chopped fresh parsley, and serve at your table with a basket of warm rolls and a fresh green salad.

Serves 4–5.

Penne Mediterraneo

Here, penne pasta is seductively infused with the Mediterranean flavors of garlic, lemon, pine nuts, and fresh mint, creating an irresistibly fragrant dish that is perfect for a romantic dinner. Place irises or lilies on the table in honor of Juno, the Roman Goddess of love and marriage.

1 pound Italian penne pasta
3 tablespoons extra-virgin olive oil
1 medium onion, diced
6 garlic cloves, minced
¼ teaspoon chili flakes
1 medium zucchini, sliced into half-moons
1 cup roasted sliced red peppers
2 tablespoons lemon juice
½ cup dry white wine
⅔ cup chopped fresh mint
¼ cup pine nuts, lightly toasted

In a large pot, bring salted water to a rolling boil to cook the penne. Heat the olive oil in a skillet and sauté the onion for 4 minutes. Add the garlic and chili flakes and stir, cooking for 1 minute. Add the zucchini and sauté until tender-crisp, about 5 minutes. Add the roasted peppers, lemon juice, white wine, and mint and bring to a simmer. Cover and remove from heat. Let sit for 10–15 minutes, while the pasta cooks until it is al dente.

Drain the cooked pasta and pour into a warmed pasta bowl. Combine with the vegetables and mix well. Sprinkle with toasted pine nuts. Serve immediately with soft, fresh pita bread and chilled white wine.

Serves 4 (or 2, for a romantic dinner with plenty of leftovers).

Tortellini with Sun-Dried Tomatoes and Feta

The intensely deep character of sun-dried tomatoes is another one of life's great pleasures. Serve this delectable tortellini in honor of the Roman Goddess Fortuna, who stands atop the Wheel of Fate. Raise a glass of pinot grigio to her and toss in extra parsley for luck.

1	pound cheese-filled tortellini
20	sun-dried tomatoes (dry-packed)
4–6	tablespoons extra-virgin olive oil
6	garlic cloves, minced
4	scallions, sliced diagonally
2	tablespoons capers, rinsed
2	teaspoons balsamic vinegar
¼	cup chopped fresh Italian parsley
1	teaspoon marjoram
16	kalamata olives
	Black pepper, freshly ground
6	ounces feta cheese, crumbled

In a large pot, bring salted water to a rolling boil and cook the tortellini until al dente. In a bowl, pour boiling water over sun-dried tomatoes and allow them to soak for 10–15 minutes, until they are soft. Drain them, reserving a ½ cup of the liquid. Chop the tomatoes and set aside.

In a skillet, heat the olive oil over low-medium heat and lightly sauté the tomatoes, garlic, scallions, and capers for about 4–5 minutes. Add the tomato water, balsamic vinegar, parsley, marjoram, olives, and black pepper. Heat through for about 3 minutes.

Drain the cooked tortellini and pour into a warmed serving bowl. Add the skillet sauce mixture and crumbled feta and toss well. Serve immediately with some freshly baked corn muffins and chilled white wine.

Serves 4–6.

Serving idea

- You may also enjoy this, cooled to room temperature, as a pasta salad.

Spinach and Feta Calzone

Calzones are virtually stuffed breads that can be filled with any assortment of vegetables and cheeses. They also make terrific picnic food, as they are easy to prepare ahead of time and travel very well. So pack some up and go for a hike. Artemis would approve.

1 teaspoon active dry yeast
¾ cup warm water
¾ teaspoon salt
¾ teaspoon sugar
2 cups unbleached flour
2 teaspoons extra-virgin olive oil
1 tablespoon extra-virgin olive oil
1 medium onion, diced
4 garlic cloves, minced
1 bunch spinach, washed, stemmed
1 teaspoon marjoram
  Salt
  Black pepper, freshly ground
  Red pepper flakes
¾ cup feta cheese, crumbled

Bread machine: Place the dough ingredients (yeast through 2 teaspoons olive oil) into your bread machine in the order your manufacturer recommends. Choose "medium" loaf and the "dough" cycle.

By hand: Dissolve yeast in warm water and add salt, sugar, flour, and 2 teaspoons oil. Follow the "by hand" directions for kneading and rising in the *Pizza Dough* recipe (Spring, page 26).

Place the risen dough on a floured board. Gently stretch and shape the dough into a 10 to 14-inch square, and let it rest while you make the filling.

Preheat your oven to 350 degrees. Heat 1 tablespoon olive oil in a medium skillet over medium heat and sauté the onion for 5 minutes. Add the minced garlic and cook for 3 minutes. Add the spinach leaves and toss them in the oil. Lightly cook until wilted. Set aside to cool.

Take your square of dough and spoon the vegetable filling down the center. Sprinkle with herbs, sea salt, and freshly ground pepper. Add a pinch of red pepper flakes and top with crumbled feta.

Fold over one side of the dough to cover the filling, like a blanket, and fold the opposite side over the first side. Pinch and seal the ends and seal any seams.

Bake in a 350 degree oven for 20–30 minutes, until the bread is baked to a golden brown. Let it cool. Serve at room temperature, slicing the calzone into 2-inch servings.

Serves 4.

Grilled Polenta with Roasted Spring Vegetables

Celebrate Earth Day with the beauty of these colorful roasted vegetables served on a bed of golden polenta. If you are busy planting a tree or tackling spring chores, roast the vegetables ahead of time and serve them at room temperature. Make more than you think you'll need, because you'll wish you had some for leftovers the next day.

1	large Vidalia or sweet onion, sliced into broad pieces
1	large red pepper, cored, seeded, sliced
1	small bunch spring asparagus, tough stems removed
5	carrots, peeled, sliced diagonally
1	small head raddichio, sliced
2	cups mushrooms, halved
4–5	tablespoons extra-virgin olive oil
5	garlic cloves, sliced
2	teaspoons marjoram
¼	teaspoon rosemary
	Sea salt
	Polenta, cooled, sliced
4	ounces chèvre goat cheese or feta cheese

Preheat your oven to 350 degrees. In a large roasting pan, combine all of the cut vegetables with the olive oil, herbs, and sea salt, tossing to coat. Roast in the oven for 45–55 minutes, or until the veggies are fork-tender. Set aside.

Reset oven temperature to broil. Place the *Polenta* slices (Autumn, page 123, or use commercially prepared) on a broiler pan or baking sheet, brush lightly with olive oil, and broil for 3–5 minutes, until the edges begin to brown. Remove from the oven.

To serve, place two or three polenta slices on each plate. Top with roasted vegetables and slices of goat cheese.

Serves 4.

Serving ideas

- Serve with a salad plate of baby spring greens garnished with hard-boiled egg wedges and dressed in *Dijon Vinaigrette* (Winter, page 185).
- If you've made enough for leftovers, simply warm gently in a nonstick skillet and share with someone you love, sitting out on the back porch and breathing in the scent of spring.

Pizza Dough

Many Goddesses make their pizza dough in a bread machine, which makes it easy to have fresh dough on hand for homemade pizza. You can certainly put this together without one and knead the dough yourself, however.

1½	teaspoons dry active yeast
1¾	cups warm water
1½	teaspoons sea salt
2	tablespoons honey
4	tablespoons olive oil
1	tablespoon Italian herbs
4	cups unbleached flour
2	tablespoons cornmeal

Bread machine: Place the ingredients in your bread machine in the order suggested by the manufacturer. Set on "large loaf," "dough" cycle. When cycle is complete, remove dough and punch down.

By hand: Dissolve yeast in water with salt and honey. Add in the oil, herbs, flour, and cornmeal. Form dough into a ball. Knead for 10 minutes and smooth into a ball. Place in an oiled bowl and cover with oiled plastic wrap. Let rise for 1½ hours. Punch down.

Divide the dough in half, if two round pizzas are desired (if you want one large rectangle pizza, do not divide). Roll out and stretch each half to about 12 inches. Cover and let rest 10 minutes.

If you are using a pizza pan, sprinkle it with cornmeal. Lay the dough on the pan. (If you are using a pizza stone, lay your dough on a well-floured peel and preheat your stone in the oven.) Let the dough rest while you create your topping.

Makes two 10 to 12-inch pizzas.

Serving ideas
- Use the prepared dough to make *Paradise Pizza* (Spring, page 27), *Spinach and Feta Calzone* (Spring, page 24), *Yellow Tomato and Portobello Mushroom Pizza* (Summer, page 73), *Roasted Vegetable Pizza* (Autumn, page 132), or *Mushroom Marinara Calzone* (Winter, page 176.)

Paradise Pizza

Inspired by the tropical pleasures exalted in the Goddess-like Tahitian paintings by the French artist Paul Gauguin, I searched for a combination of flavors invoking paradise—pleasure for both the palate and the eye.

1   tablespoon extra-virgin olive oil

1   small Bermuda or red onion, sliced

6   garlic cloves, sliced

1   sweet red pepper, cored, seeded, sliced

Prepared *Pizza Dough*, stretched and rolled out

¼–½   cup prepared pesto

5   pineapple rings, drained

2–3   tablespoons chopped fresh basil or cilantro

4   ounces chèvre goat cheese or feta cheese, cubed

Red pepper flakes or fennel seeds

Preheat your oven to 400 degrees. In a medium-sized skillet, heat the olive oil over medium heat and sauté the onion for 5 minutes. Add the garlic and red pepper and stir-fry for 5 minutes, until tender-crisp. Remove from heat.

Spoon the pesto thinly over the *Pizza Dough* (Spring, page 26). Arrange the cooked onions, garlic, and peppers evenly across the pizza. Add the pineapple rings and sprinkle with basil or cilantro. Dot with cubes of goat cheese. Dash on hot pepper flakes, if desired, or fennel. Drizzle the edge of the crust with a little extra-virgin olive oil.

Bake for 15–20 minutes, until the pizza crust is nicely browned. Serve with a crisp green salad garnished with chilled Mandarin orange slices tossed in *Ginger Dressing* (Summer, page 87).

Serves 2–4.

Huevos Rancheros

Celebrate fertility Southwestern-style. The Corn Mother spices her eggs up with the fire of chiles and the grounding energy of black beans on a corn tortilla.

1 tablespoon extra-virgin olive oil

4 corn tortillas

1 can (1 pound) black beans, drained, rinsed (or favorite refried beans)

¼ teaspoon chili powder

½ teaspoon cumin

8 free-range eggs or egg substitute

Sea salt

Black pepper, freshly ground

1 cup *Garlic Salsa*

½ cup green chiles

¾ cup grated jack cheese, crumbled feta, or soy cheese

Green Goddess Guacamole

Light sour cream or soy equivalent

Fresh cilantro, chopped

Preheat your oven to 400 degrees. Heat a tablespoon of olive oil in a large nonstick skillet and lightly fry the tortillas until they are soft. Drain them on paper towels. In a saucepan, gently heat through the black beans, stirring in chili powder and cumin.

Prepare the eggs in the nonstick skillet, traditional style—sunny side up or over easy. Season with sea salt and freshly ground pepper.

Arrange the tortillas on oiled ovenproof plates. Spoon ¼ of the warmed beans onto each tortilla, then spread ¼ cup *Garlic Salsa* (Summer, page 54). Next, add two cooked eggs and top with green chiles and grated cheese.

Bake in the upper half of your oven, just enough to melt the cheese and warm the dish through, about 5 minutes.

Serve with *Green Goddess Guacamole* (Summer, page 53), light sour cream, and a garnish of fresh chopped cilantro.

Serves 4.

Fettuccine with Asparagus and Lemon

This lovely spring pasta features tender young asparagus spears (thought to be an aphrodisiac!) and a light lemony sauce on a bed of fettuccine.

1   pound Italian fettuccine

3   tablespoons extra-virgin olive oil

4   garlic cloves, minced

2   cups tender asparagus spears, tough ends removed

2   tablespoons capers, rinsed

2   tablespoons lemon juice

2   tablespoons dry white wine

1   teaspoon grated lemon peel

½   cup soy or dairy cream

¼   cup grated Asiago or Pecorino cheese

    White pepper, freshly ground

2   tablespoons chopped fresh parsley

Boil fresh water in a large pot for the fettuccine, and cook the pasta till al dente. In a large skillet, heat the olive oil over medium heat and sauté the garlic for 1 minute. Slice the asparagus spears, diagonally, into 3-inch pieces and toss in with the garlic. Add the capers and lemon juice and sauté for 4–5 minutes, just until the asparagus is tender-crisp. Add wine, lemon peel, and cream. Stir well until heated through. (Do not overcook the asparagus.)

When the pasta is done, drain and pour it into a warmed pasta serving bowl. Drizzle with a little extra-virgin olive oil, add the cheese and freshly ground white pepper, and toss well. Add the asparagus and sauce from the skillet and toss together.

Garnish with the fresh parsley and serve at the table Italian-style, with a salad of baby greens and *Lemon-Garlic Vinaigrette* (Spring, page 39).

Serves 4.

Lemon Risotto with Baby Peas

Here is a delicious risotto for Beltane . . . arborio rice (for fertility) laced with a spring-like infusion of lemon (for longevity) and green onions.

2	tablespoons extra-virgin olive oil
½	cup green onions, sliced diagonally
2	teaspoons grated lemon zest
1½	cups Italian arborio rice, uncooked
2	tablespoons lemon juice
½	cup white wine
5	cups light vegetable broth, heated
¾	cup baby peas, fresh (parboil first), or frozen
¼	cup grated Parmesan cheese
2	tablespoons half-and-half (optional)
2	tablespoons chopped fresh Italian parsley

In a heavy saucepan, heat the olive oil over medium heat and sauté the onions and lemon zest for about 5 minutes. Add the uncooked arborio rice and stir for about 1 minute. Add the lemon juice and wine and stir, cooking until the liquid reduces, about 5 minutes.

Add in 2 cups of the vegetable broth and bring to a simmer, stirring constantly until the liquid has been absorbed, about 7 minutes. Add in the remaining broth, one cup at a time, stirring until each cup of broth is absorbed before adding the next. Add in the peas with the fourth cup of broth. (This whole process should take about 20 minutes.)

When the final cup of liquid has been absorbed, add the Parmesan and stir until the rice is creamy but still retains some "bite." Stir in 2 tablespoons of half-and-half, if desired, and the fresh chopped parsley. Remove from heat and let stand for several moments before serving.

Warm up four serving bowls. Spoon the risotto into the warm bowls and garnish with some more fresh chopped parsley.

Serves 4.

Savory Sides

Tofu Scramble

All Goddesses like to stir things up. Awaken your protein with the aromatic fire of garlic, ginger, and chiles. You'll increase your energy and protect your heart.

2–3 tablespoons extra-virgin olive oil
1 Vidalia onion, cut into chunks
5 garlic cloves, minced
½ teaspoon ginger
½ teaspoon chili powder
½ yellow pepper, seeded, chopped
1 cup sliced shiitake mushrooms
4 roma tomatoes, chopped
1 pound extra-firm tofu, drained (if packed wet), cut into bite-size pieces
2 tablespoons tamari or soy sauce
White pepper, freshly ground
Fresh chives, chopped
4 tortillas, warmed
Spanish Rice

Heat the olive oil over medium heat in a large skillet and sauté the onion for 5 minutes until softened. Add the garlic and spices, stir, and cook 1 minute. Add the pepper and mushrooms, stir-frying until tender-crisp. Add the tomatoes and slices of tofu. Gently stir-fry for 3–4 minutes. Sprinkle with tamari sauce and freshly ground white pepper.

Serve on a warm plate with a folded warm tortilla and a spoonful of *Spanish Rice* (Autumn, page 135). *Serves 4.*

Serving idea
- Try it with a spoonful of *Couscous* (Autumn, page 131) and some warm pita bread.

Spring Asparagus with White Bean Sauce

Life is short . . . and so is the season for tender young asparagus! Take advantage of this spring treasure and try it served in a variety of ways. Here I have topped the delicate spears with a creamy, savory sauce that's also high in protein.

1	tablespoon extra-virgin olive oil
4	garlic cloves, crushed
½	teaspoon curry powder
½	teaspoon fennel
1	can (1 pound) northern white (cannellini) beans, drained, rinsed
2–4	tablespoons vegetable broth or bouillon (just enough to thin the sauce)
2	tablespoons white wine or dry vermouth
	Sea salt
	White pepper, freshly ground
1	tablespoon extra-virgin olive oil
1	bunch young asparagus, tough stems removed
1	tablespoon lemon juice
	Sea salt
	White pepper, freshly ground

To make the sauce, heat the olive oil in a skillet over low-medium heat and sauté the garlic for 1 minute. Add the curry powder and fennel and stir, cooking for 1 minute. Pour in the beans and stir to coat them evenly. Add sea salt and white pepper to taste. Remove from heat.

Spoon about half of the bean mixture into a blender with a tablespoon of the vegetable broth and white wine. Cover and purée 2–3 minutes. Add the remaining beans and a bit more liquid. Cover and purée again, scraping down the sides of the blender, if you need to. Adjust the liquid until the white bean sauce is at the desired consistency. Pour the mixture into a sauce pan and heat through gently.

To prepare the asparagus, heat 1 tablespoon of olive oil in a skillet over medium heat and add the asparagus. Lightly sauté 2–3 minutes. Sprinkle with lemon juice, sea salt, and ground pepper, cooking until just tender-crisp, about 2–3 more minutes. Do not overcook.

Serve immediately on a warm plate, topped with warm white bean sauce.

Serves 4.

Roasted Vegetable Ratatouille

Roasting the traditional ratatouille vegetables first adds a deeper, smoky flavor to this quintessential vegetarian dish. Serve it with steamed basmati rice, crusty French bread, and a glass of your favorite French merlot.

1 onion, cut into chunks

1 large eggplant, peeled, cubed

1 red bell pepper, cored, seeded, julienned

1 green bell pepper, cored, seeded, julienned

1 medium zucchini, sliced into half-moons

1 pound roma tomatoes, sliced in half lengthwise

3 tablespoons extra-virgin olive oil

4 garlic cloves, crushed

1 teaspoon Italian herbs

2 tablespoons chopped fresh Italian parsley

2 tablespoons chopped fresh basil

Sea salt

Black pepper, freshly ground

1 tablespoon olive oil

3 tablespoons balsamic vinegar

½ cup sliced black olives

2 tablespoons capers, rinsed

½ cup red wine

Preheat your oven to 375 degrees. Combine all of the vegetables in an oiled roasting pan and toss with the olive oil, garlic, herbs, sea salt, and pepper. Roast them at the top of your oven for about 30 minutes, until the veggies are tender and slightly charred at the edges.

In a large skillet, heat 1 tablespoon olive oil over medium heat and add the roasted vegetables along with the vinegar, olives, capers, and wine. Cover and simmer on low for about 10 minutes, until the liquid is reduced and the flavors are mingled.

Serve hot over steamed basmati rice or at room temperature with *Crostini* (Winter, page 154) and a crisp green salad.

Serves 4.

Serving idea

- Try it spooned into a bowl of soft, warm polenta. (See recipe for *Country-style Garlic Polenta*, Autumn, page 123).

Marinated Grilled Vegetables

Fire up the grill for this favorite time of year and roast an assortment of vegetables marinated in balsamic vinegar and garlic.

2   sweet onions, peeled,
    sliced in chunks

2   sweet bell peppers,
    seeded, sliced

2   red peppers, seeded,
    sliced

2   large portobello
    mushroom caps, sliced

1   medium eggplant, sliced
    into rounds, halved

¾   cup extra-virgin olive oil

½   cup balsamic vinegar

6–8 garlic cloves, minced

1   teaspoon Italian herbs

2   sprigs fresh rosemary
    Sea salt
    Black pepper, freshly
    ground

Preheat the grill to medium heat. In a large bowl, combine all of the vegetables. Make your marinade in a large measuring cup, combining the oil, vinegar, garlic, and Italian herbs. Pour the marinade over the vegetables and gently mix to coat. Allow the vegetables to sit for 45 minutes to 1 hour.

Using a double thickness of heavy-duty aluminum foil, cut a large square to hold the vegetables. Place the foil on a cookie sheet for support. Spoon the vegetables onto the center of the foil and even them out. Add the rosemary sprigs. Cut another piece of foil for the top and seal in the vegetables.

When the fire is hot, move the foil packet carefully onto the grill and lower the cover. Grill the vegetables for at least 20 minutes, depending on the heat of the fire and the size of your grill. Sneak a peek now and then to make sure they aren't scorching too much on the bottom. Move them around with a wooden spoon if you have to. When the vegetables are tender, remove the packet to a large platter and open.

Serve directly from the foil as an appetizer or side dish. Wonderful served with a loaf of bread and a plate of soft goat cheese!

Serves 6.

Sautéed Cabbage with Toasted Walnuts

The sweet crunch of sautéed cabbage is perfectly complemented by aromatic balsamic vinegar and the warmth of toasted walnuts in this simple dish, perfect on the night of the Storm Moon.

Olive oil spray
½ cup sliced walnuts
3–4 tablespoons extra-virgin olive oil
4 garlic cloves, minced
1 white cabbage, cored, finely shredded
3 tablespoons balsamic vinegar
4 garlic cloves, minced
Sea salt
White pepper, freshly ground

Spray a large nonstick skillet with olive oil and heat over medium heat. Add the walnuts and toast them lightly for 2–3 minutes. Remove them with a spatula and set aside.

Add the olive oil to the skillet and heat, then add the garlic and sauté until it becomes golden. Add the shredded cabbage and balsamic vinegar, raise the heat, and stir-fry for 1 minute or so. The cabbage should be tender-crisp and hot.

Toss in the toasted walnuts and season to taste with sea salt and freshly ground pepper.

Serves 4–6.

Serving idea

• Serve as a side dish with brown rice and hummus, calzones, or burritos.

Spring Salads

Roasted Two Potato Salad

Combining sweet potatoes with white potatoes gives classic potato salad a new flavor twist. Serve these potatoes on a full moon and celebrate your potential.

2	tablespoons extra-virgin olive oil
2	large sweet potatoes, peeled, cubed
4	medium new potatoes, peeled, cubed
½	cup extra-virgin olive oil
¼	cup balsamic vinegar
¼	teaspoon fennel
	Sea salt
	Black pepper, freshly ground
½	cup chopped green onions
¾	cup chopped celery
¼	cup chopped fresh parsley

Preheat your oven to 400 degrees. Toss the sweet and new potatoes in a clay baking dish with 2 tablespoons extra-virgin olive oil and a dash of sea salt. Cover and roast for 20–30 minutes, until the potatoes are fork-tender. Place the potatoes in a serving bowl.

As they cool, whisk together the ½ cup of extra-virgin olive oil with balsamic vinegar. Add the fennel. Season the potatoes with sea salt and freshly ground pepper, to taste. Add in the chopped green onions, celery, and fresh parsley.

Pour the dressing over the warm potatoes and gently mix with a wooden spoon. Serve at room temperature. If not serving immediately, cover and chill.

Serves 4.

Tofu Salad

For those Vegan Goddesses who don't eat eggs, here is a healthy alternative to the classic egg salad. Even if you do eat eggs, try this yummy salad for a change of pace, stuffed into fresh pita bread. Venus would have eaten hers with plenty of fresh juicy tomatoes!

1	package firm tofu, pressed and drained in a colander
½	medium red onion, chopped fine
1	celery stalk, chopped
2–3	tablespoons soy mayonnaise or egg mayonnaise
1½	teaspoons Dijon mustard
1	teaspoon curry powder
1	teaspoon dill
	Sea salt
	Black pepper, freshly ground
	Pita bread
	Sprouts or salad greens
	Cucumbers, sliced
	Cherry tomatoes, halved

In a mixing bowl, chop up the tofu with a fork into small pieces. Add the onion, celery, mayonnaise, Dijon mustard, curry, dill, and salt and pepper. Mix well, cover, and refrigerate until serving.

Serve in pita bread pockets with sprouts or baby greens, sliced cucumbers, and cherry tomato halves.

Lemon-Garlic Vinaigrette

A light, lemony vinaigrette that is perfect for spring greens.

2 tablespoons lemon juice

½ teaspoon grated lemon peel

2 tablespoons extra-virgin olive oil

1 teaspoon white wine vinegar

1 garlic clove, minced

1 teaspoon mint, chopped

1 tablespoon fresh parsley, finely chopped

Combine all the ingredients and serve immediately. Makes a lively spring salad with mixed bitter greens.

Serving idea

- To liven things ups, try adding ⅓ cup chilled cooked peas, 8–10 marinated artichoke hearts, and 2–3 red, spicy radishes, sliced.

Tomatoes in Creamy Lime and Chili Dressing

Aphrodite's fruit of love—the juicy red tomato—drizzled with a savory lime and chili dressing . . . a cool accompaniment for your Beltane feast.

4   ripe fresh tomatoes, washed, sliced
¾   cup fat-free sour cream or plain yogurt
    Juice of 2 limes
1   Anaheim chili pepper, seeded, finely chopped
1   garlic clove, minced
    Cumin
2   tablespoons finely chopped cilantro
    White pepper, freshly ground
    Fresh cilantro, chopped

Arrange sliced tomatoes on a chilled plate. Combine the remaining ingredients in a small bowl and whisk well until smooth and creamy. Taste for seasoning adjustments. Drizzle the dressing over the tomatoes. Sprinkle extra chopped cilantro all over the plate for flourish.

Serves 4.

Serving idea

• Try this salad dressing on fresh spinach leaves, garnished with thinly sliced red onion, chilled chickpeas, and chunks of juicy cucumbers.

Sweet Endings

Banana Chip Ice Cream

Use only ripe flavorful bananas in this subtle frozen confection. The chocolate chips can be optional, but my family wouldn't ever let me leave them out.

½ cup half-and-half or soy cream

2 cups milk or almond milk

2 ripe bananas, peeled, sliced

1 cup sugar or ½ cup honey

2 teaspoons Mexican vanilla extract

¼ teaspoon xanthan gum (optional)

½ cup gourmet chocolate chips (optional)

Combine the cream and milk in a blender with the banana slices, sugar, and vanilla. Cover and whip until the sugar is dissolved. Add the xanthan gum and whip until smooth and frothy. Pour into your ice cream maker and add the chocolate chips, if desired. Freeze according to the manufacturer's instructions.

Take your banana treat out onto the back porch and enjoy the spreading warmth of the longer spring evenings . . . and listen for the peepers.

Serves 4–5.

Chocolate-Almond Coconut Ice Cream

The sensual combination of coconut and chocolate makes this frozen dessert a Goddess favorite.

2 cups coconut milk
½ cup half-and-half (optional)
1 cup sugar
2 teaspoons Mexican vanilla extract
½ teaspoon coconut extract (optional)
¼ teaspoon xanthan gum (optional)
½ cup flaked coconut
¼ cup gourmet chocolate chips
⅓ cup almond slivers, toasted

Combine the coconut milk, half-and-half, and sugar in a blender. Cover and whip until the sugar is dissolved. Add the flavor extracts and xanthan gum and whip until smooth and frothy. Pour into your ice cream maker and stir in the coconut, chocolate chips, and almonds. Freeze according to the manufacturer's instructions. Dig in immediately!

Serves 4–5.

Golden Carrot Cake

An ideal dessert for the rites of Spring, this sweet and spicy carrot cake has been my favorite cake recipe for years. Everyone has their own special carrot cake formula, so here is mine.

3 cups organic unbleached flour

1 teaspoon baking soda

1 teaspoon baking powder

¼ teaspoon sea salt

¼ cup canola oil

4 free-range eggs, beaten

1 cup honey

½ cup plain yogurt

3 cups grated carrots

½ cup golden raisins

½ cup chopped pecans

½ cup flaked coconut

¾ cup crushed pineapple, drained

1 teaspoon vanilla extract

1 teaspoon cinnamon

¼ teaspoon nutmeg

½ teaspoon allspice

Orange Cream Cheese Icing

¾ cup honey

12 ounces light cream cheese or Neufchâtel

½ teaspoon vanilla extract

1 teaspoon orange extract

1 teaspoon fine orange zest

½ cup flaked coconut

Preheat oven to 325 degrees. Sift together the dry ingredients: flour, baking soda, baking powder, and sea salt. In a separate bowl, beat together the canola oil and eggs. Add the honey, yogurt, carrots, raisins, pecans, coconut, pineapple, vanilla, and spices. Add the dry ingredients to the wet mixture and stir well, making sure the batter is well blended.

Bake in two greased and floured 8-inch cake pans for about 1 hour plus, until the cake is done. The center should spring back when touched. Cool on wire rack for 45 minutes before removing cakes from pans. When the cakes are cooled, cover with *Orange Cream Cheese Icing* (below).

Serves 6–8.

Orange Cream Cheese Icing

In a mixing bowl, beat the honey, cream cheese, extracts, and zest together until smooth. Place one cake layer on a serving plate and cover with less than half of the icing. Place the second cake directly on top of the frosted layer and ice this layer completely. Garnish with the flaked coconut.

Bear Dreamer's Walnut Biscotti

This recipe was created by my friend Nancy, a Bear Dreamer. Try these crisp biscotti dipped in your favorite coffee or tea for a midafternoon pick-me-up. (And don't forget to leave a little milk and biscotti for the faeries on May 4, the Day of Faeries!)

1 cup sugar
3 eggs
2 egg whites
⅛ cup canola oil
2 teaspoons vanilla
      extract
2 cups unbleached
      all-purpose flour
1 teaspoon baking
      powder
¼ teaspoon salt
1 cup coarsely chopped
      walnuts

Preheat your oven to 350 degrees. In a mixing bowl, cream the sugar with the eggs and oil, until the mixture is smooth and the sugar is dissolved. Stir in the vanilla. In a separate large bowl, combine all of the dry ingredients. Using a wooden spoon, stir the dry and wet ingredients together until the dough is mixed.

Spoon the dough out onto a lightly greased baking sheet, making a long loaf shape, about 4 to 5 inches in width. Sprinkle some flour over the loaf and smooth the dough with your hands, pressing down to flatten it, creating a long, even shape. Make the surface as smooth as possible.

Place in the oven and bake for 20–25 minutes. Remove from the oven and set it aside to cool for about 5 minutes.

Using a large, sharp serrated knife, carefully slice across the loaf at a slight diagonal, at about ½-inch intervals. Place these biscotti back onto the baking sheet and return to the oven. Continue baking for another 5 minutes. Turn the biscotti over and bake for another 5 minutes, if necessary, until they are crisp. Remove the biscotti to a wire rack to cool. Store in an airtight container.

Note: For chocolate-walnut biscotti, add 3 tablespoons unsweetened cocoa to the flour mixture.

Makes approximately 20 biscotti.

Notes on your favorite Spring recipes

By summer the Goddess is abundant, in full bloom, **radiant**. She is Hera, wife and mother, mature, strong, and nurturing. Standing in the south, she is adorned in **red**. At the height of her powers, she is **fire** and will. The Queen and The Lady, Isis and Eve; we revel in her **bounty** and warmth and receive her nourishment with gratitude.

It is a time of immersion in the natural world. In growing our **gardens** of vegetables and flowers, in tending our herbs and picking our strawberries, we are in **communion** with our Mother Earth, our hands in her soil, our eyes toward the **rain clouds**. Listen to the wind in the leaves and leave little presents for the faery folk.

Summer

Festival Menus

Summer Solstice (aka Midsummer)

The longest day of the year falls at about June 21. This is midsummer, a time for weddings and celebrations of transition. The Goddess is ripe and voluptuous. Roses are in bloom, the birds sing early, the sun is high in the sky. Ishtar, the Great Goddess, reigns over love and war. The Babylonian Creatrix, she embodies the source of all life, she is the Giver of Plenty. Herbs harvested on this morning, close to dawn, will hold the most potent magick of the season. Fill your table with fruit and flowers, dance to flute music, and wear the scents of rose and lavender. Rejoice in love and revel in beauty.

Wine Cooler Punch *(page 51)*

Marinated Olives *(page 52)*

Basil-Infused Olive Oil *(page 55)* with Rosemary Focaccia *(pages 56–57)*

Chilled Potato Leek Soup *(page 60)*

Garden Vegetable Linguini with Mint *(page 65)*

Curried Slaw *(page 88)*

Lavender Cookies *(page 94)* with Orange Sherbet with Chocolate Chips *(page 93)*

First Harvest (aka Lughnasadh)

In honor of Lugh, the God of light, fire, and the sun, consort of the Great Mother Goddess, the Celts created their most important fire festival of the year. At the time of the first harvest, it becomes evident how easy or hard the coming winter will be, based on the success or failure of the grain crop. Spirits are high, rejoicing as the first harvest is brought in.

On Lammas, August 2, we celebrate the Feast of Bread. Fill an earthenware jug with sunflowers and light candles of orange and gold. Bake a loaf of bread and leave some outside at dawn, in offering to Lugh. Plant seeds today from fruit you have eaten, symbolizing your understanding of the cycle of birth, death, and rebirth. Burn a braid of dried sweetgrass to cleanse your home so that the Goddess might bring sweetness into your life.

Sun-Dried Tomato and Basil Pesto *(page 58)*
Southwestern Polenta *(pages 68–69)*
Fresh Summer Greens and Grapes in a Basil-Citrus Vinaigrette *(page 89)*
Amen Farm Apple Cake *(page 95)*

Beverages and Bites

Wine Cooler Punch

On this festival of the longest sun, refresh yourself with a light libation of chilled white wine with a splash of effervescence and fruit.

1   bottle of chilled white wine, such as chardonnay or pinot grigio

1   cup chilled fruit juice, such as pear or white grape

1   bottle chilled sparkling mineral water, flavored with lemon or lime

1   lemon, washed, sliced into rounds

1   lime, washed, sliced into rounds

Fill a punch bowl with the chilled wine, about a cup of juice, and a bottle of the sparkling mineral water. Stir and taste for adjustments. Add in the sliced fruit for color and flavor. I recommend at least doubling this recipe for any serious reveling!

Serves 4–6.

Marinated Olives

Olives, the gift from Athena, Goddess of Agriculture, are easy to marinate. Create your own marinated olives and enjoy them at your leisure. After all, aren't such pleasures what summertime is all about?

1 pound dry- (or oil-) cured black olives

1 pound assorted olives (such as Ionian, green, kalamata), drained

¼ cup extra-virgin olive oil

¼ cup balsamic vinegar

5 garlic cloves, minced

2 tablespoons chopped fresh Italian parsley

¼ teaspoon marjoram
   Fresh rosemary sprigs, stripped
   Black pepper, freshly ground

Place all the olives in an airtight storage container. Combine the marinade ingredients in a measuring cup and pour the marinade over the olives. Cover and chill for several hours; overnight is even better. Serve the olives at room temperature.

Green Goddess Guacamole

Revel in the green season and make a fresh guacamole any Venus would be proud of. Serve it with organic blue corn tortilla chips . . . the dark blue color against the ripe green of the avocado is striking.

2 ripe avocados, peeled, pitted

2 red ripe tomatoes, chopped

3 garlic cloves, minced

Juice from half a lemon

½ teaspoon cumin

¼ cup fresh finely chopped cilantro

Chili flakes

Sea salt

Black pepper, freshly ground

1 bag organic blue corn tortilla chips

Mash the avocados in a bowl and add the chopped tomatoes, garlic, lemon juice, cumin, and cilantro. Season with chili flakes, sea salt, and black pepper, to taste. Mix until well blended. Cover and chill if not serving immediately. Serve in the center of a generous ring of organic blue corn chips.

Serves 4–6.

Garlic Salsa

As a festive Southwestern dip for tortilla chips or a spicy addition to a burrito, salsas add a big flavor kick to any dish. This one, my favorite, features garlic, of course—a Goddess staple.

2   cups chopped roma tomatoes
1   small red onion, diced fine
6   garlic cloves, minced
1   red pepper, seeded, cored, chopped
2   jalapeño peppers, seeded (or keep seeds for more heat), chopped
1   can (14 ounces) Mexican-style tomatoes
2   tablespoons balsamic vinegar
¼   cup lime juice
⅔   cup fresh chopped cilantro
1   teaspoon cumin
1   teaspoon hot chili powder or cayenne pepper

Combine all of the ingredients, cover, and let stand for an hour so that all the flavors mingle. Taste for seasoning adjustments.

Serve at room temperature. Refrigerate if you are not going to serve it right away. Homemade salsa usually keeps well refrigerated for up to 4 days (if it doesn't disappear first).

Basil-Infused Olive Oil

Fruity extra-virgin olive oil infused with fresh sweet basil from the garden is exotically delicious. We enjoy our basil olive oil with fresh warm bread at the table, dipping into a communal saucer.

1 cup extra-virgin olive oil

6–8 fresh sweet basil leaves

Pour the olive oil into a small saucepan with the basil leaves and gently heat the oil over low heat for about 15 minutes. Remove from heat and set aside to cool to room temperature. Store in a pretty, corked bottle or pottery oil decanter.

For serving, pour the room-temperature oil into a saucer plate, leaving behind the basil leaves, or store in an airtight container at room temperature.

Serving ideas

- Try using the basil-infused oil to add extra flavor to your pasta dishes.
- Drizzle it on vegetables, focaccia, or pizza.
- For a change, try adding fresh cloves of garlic or other herbs to your oil, such as rosemary or Greek oregano.

Rosemary Focaccia

This rustic and dense bread is full of flavor and texture. Served warm and drizzled with basil-infused olive oil, it can give any Goddess visions of Italy! Cut into squares, sliced in half, and filled, it makes a delicious Italian-style sandwich.

1½ teaspoons dry active yeast
3 cups unbleached flour
1 tablespoon cornmeal
1 teaspoon salt
1 tablespoon honey
3 tablespoons extra-virgin olive oil
1¼ cup warm water
1 teaspoon dried minced garlic (or fresh)
1 tablespoon dried onion flakes
2 tablespoons Italian herbs
1 teaspoon fresh rosemary
1 teaspoon red pepper flakes
2 tablespoons extra-virgin olive oil
1 teaspoon fresh rosemary
Coarse salt

Note: The following instructions are for using a bread machine. If you do not use one to make your dough, please refer to the *Sun-Dried Tomato Focaccia* recipe (Spring, pages 12–13) and follow the "by hand" instructions.

Add the ingredients (from yeast through red pepper flakes) into your bread machine according to your manufacturer's instructions. Choose the "dough" setting.

When the dough cycle is complete, turn the dough out onto a board dusted with cornmeal, cover, and let it rest 10 minutes. Sprinkle the dough with cornmeal, flatten and roll it out with a rolling pin, or your hands, to a 12 to 14-inch oval or circle.

Sprinkle cornmeal on a baking sheet and place the focaccia dough on the pan. Brush the surface with 1 tablespoon extra-virgin olive oil and cover with a clean towel, letting it rise for 20 minutes, or until doubled in height. (If you are using a pizza stone, place the dough on a peel dusted with cornmeal, brush with oil, cover with a clean towel, and preheat the stone in the oven for 20 minutes, while the dough is rising.)

Preheat your oven to 450 degrees. When the dough has risen, use your finger to dimple the focaccia surface all over. Sprinkle with a teaspoon of rosemary. Drizzle with extra-virgin olive oil and

continued

sprinkle with coarse salt. Place the focaccia in the upper half of your oven. (If you are using a pizza stone, sprinkle it now with some cornmeal, and slide the focaccia dough from the peel onto the stone.)

Bake at 450 degrees for 10 minutes, then reduce heat to 350 degrees and continue baking for 12–15 minutes, until the bread is golden brown. Remove from the oven and cool on a wire rack.

Serve warm or at room temperature, sliced into wedges, with a saucer of *Basil-Infused Olive Oil* (Summer, page 55).

Sun-Dried Tomato and Basil Pesto

The combination of rich sun-dried tomatoes with refreshing summer basil makes a superior pesto spread for a summer appetizer. Spread it on toasted, crusty bread slices in honor of Lammas.

10–12   sun-dried tomatoes (dry-packed)

2   cups packed fresh basil leaves

¼   cup pine nuts or walnuts

4   garlic cloves, peeled

¼   cup grated Parmesan cheese

½   cup extra-virgin olive oil

Pour boiling water over the sun-dried tomatoes and let them steep until moistened, about 10 minutes. Drain, pat dry, and set aside.

In a food processor or blender, place the basil leaves, tomatoes, pine nuts, garlic, and Parmesan. (If you plan on freezing the pesto for future use, skip the Parmesan cheese.) Begin to process or puree, adding the olive oil a little at a time as you process, stopping to scrape down the sides as you go. Blend until the pesto is a smooth paste. Adjust the oil if it seems dry.

Cover and chill for 2 hours. Serve at room temperature on warm toasted bread.

Serving ideas

- Try it tossed with your favorite hot pasta for an instant sauce.
- Spread it on pizza dough for an incredibly delicious treat.

Seasonal Soups

Ginger Mushroom Soup

A light and delectable soup with Asian overtones, this makes an ideal supper for a Blessing Moon night. Give thanks to Gaia in her eternal glory and all her mystery.

2 tablespoons sesame oil
    or canola oil
1 small onion, finely
    chopped
5 garlic cloves, minced
2 inches fresh ginger, grated
2 celery stalks, thinly sliced
2 carrots, peeled, julienned
½ head white cabbage,
    thinly sliced
3 cups light vegetable broth
1 package shiitake
    mushrooms, stemmed,
    sliced
1 tablespoon low-sodium
    soy sauce
1 tablespoon lemon juice
1 tablespoon sherry or
    rice vinegar
2 cups fresh water, boiled
4 tablespoons light miso or
    vegetable bouillon
1 package baked tofu,
    cut into bite-size pieces
¼ cup chopped green onions

Heat the oil in a heavy soup pot and sauté the onion for 3 minutes. Add the garlic, ginger, and celery and cook for 1 minute. Add the carrots and cabbage and stir to coat well. Pour in the broth and add the mushrooms, soy sauce, lemon juice, and vinegar.

Add the miso paste to the hot water and make a broth, then add it into the pot. Stir together and bring to a high simmer. Lower the heat and gently simmer for 20–30 minutes, until the vegetables are tender-crisp. Add in the sliced tofu and heat through another 5 minutes.

Serve in colorful soup bowls and garnish with a spoonful of chopped green onions. Lovely paired with *Eastern Goddess Summer Salad* (Summer, page 87) and some freshly baked lemony muffins.

Serves 4–6.

Chilled Potato Leek Soup

Also known as vichyssoise, this quintessential summer soup is the perfect beginning to a celebration of the summer solstice. Cool and creamy, topped with fresh chives or parsley picked right out of the garden, this delightful appetizer is always a Goddess favorite.

2 tablespoons extra-virgin olive oil

1 medium Vidalia onion, diced

3 medium leeks, white parts only, chopped

4 medium potatoes, peeled, thinly sliced

4 cups light vegetable broth

Sea salt

White pepper, freshly ground

Half-and-half or nondairy cream (as needed)

Fresh chives or parsley, chopped

In a heavy soup pot, heat the olive oil over medium heat and sauté the onion for 5 minutes. Add the leeks and potatoes, stirring for 1 minute. Add the broth, sea salt, and pepper. Lower the heat and simmer for 30–40 minutes, until the potatoes are very tender and the broth is flavorful.

Ladle a portion of the soup into a blender, cover, and puree for 2–3 minutes, adding in the half-and-half to thin to the desired consistency. Pour into a storage container and repeat for the rest of the soup. Cover and chill for several hours before serving.

Serve in chilled bowls with a garnish of chopped fresh chives or parsley.

Serves 4–6.

Garden Gazpacho

An elegant soup to serve when your garden is brimming with ripe tomatoes and peppers. If you do not have a garden, take advantage of the Great Goddess' abundance at the fresh produce market.

½ cup extra-virgin olive oil
3 tablespoons lime juice
¼ cup balsamic vinegar
2 cups vegetable or tomato juice, chilled
4 large ripe tomatoes, seeded, coarsely chopped
1 large red bell pepper, seeded, cored, coarsely chopped
1 Vidalia or red onion, chopped
1 cucumber, peeled, chopped
1 yellow pepper, seeded, cored, chopped
½ cup chopped parsley
½ cup chopped cilantro leaves
4–5 garlic cloves, crushed
1 teaspoon cumin
   Cayenne pepper or paprika
   Sea salt
   Black pepper, freshly ground
   Fresh herbs

In a small bowl, whisk together the olive oil, lime juice, vinegar, and vegetable juice.

In a blender, begin to lightly purée the vegetables, herbs, garlic, and spices in small batches at a time. Be careful not to overblend, as gazpacho should be crunchy and retain some texture. Add the remaining vegetables and complete the puree.

Combine this purée in a bowl with the oil-vinegar mixture and some sea salt and ground pepper. Blend well. Cover and chill the gazpacho for at least 2–4 hours.

Serve in well-chilled bowls and garnish with fresh herbs from the garden, such as mint leaves or cilantro.

Serves 4–6.

Serving ideas

- Try a dollop of light sour cream or tangy yogurt, with a wedge of lime.
- Pass around a basket of crunchy tortilla chips.

Everyday Feasts

Colin's Tomato and Basil Pasta

Combining ripe red and yellow tomatoes with basil and garlic from our summer garden, our son Colin tossed together a colorful, fresh sauce that lured us all into the kitchen with its enticing aroma.

1	pound Italian pasta (penne or rotini)
¼	cup extra-virgin olive oil
4	ripe red tomatoes, chopped
4	ripe yellow tomatoes, chopped
5–6	garlic cloves, minced
1	handful fresh basil, shredded
1	teaspoon dried marjoram
2	tablespoons pine nuts
	Sea salt
	Black pepper, freshly ground
	Parmesan cheese, shredded

Bring a large pot of salted water to a rolling boil. Cook the pasta until al dente. Heat the olive oil gently in a saucepan. Add the tomatoes, garlic, herbs, and pine nuts. Add salt and ground pepper to taste. Stir and heat through.

When the pasta is ready, drain and drizzle with olive oil. Pour the hot pasta into a large serving bowl and toss with the fresh tomato sauce. Serve in pasta bowls with a generous spoonful of freshly shredded Parmesan cheese.

Serves 4–5.

Penne with Cannellini Beans, Garlic, and Capers

Dance under the Hay Moon after this delicious combination of fresh garlic, capers, and cannellini beans tossed with penne pasta. Add some fresh chopped roma tomatoes from your garden if you'd like to honor Venus, the evening star.

1 pound Italian penne pasta

¼ cup extra-virgin olive oil

6 garlic cloves, peeled, sliced

1 tablespoon capers, rinsed

3 tablespoons balsamic vinegar

1 can (15 ounces) cannellini or white northern beans, drained

1 can (14 ounces) chopped Italian tomatoes or chopped fresh tomatoes

1 teaspoon fresh or dried marjoram

Sea salt

Black pepper, freshly ground

2 tablespoons chopped fresh parsley

2 tablespoons shredded fresh basil leaves

Parmesan or Romano cheese, grated

Bring a large pot of salted water to a rolling boil and cook the penne until al dente. In a medium skillet, heat the olive oil over low-medium heat and warm the garlic and capers for 1–2 minutes. Add in the balsamic vinegar, beans, tomatoes, and marjoram, season with sea salt and black pepper, and bring to a gentle simmer.

When the pasta is done, drain well and pour it into a large, warmed serving bowl. Add the skillet mixture along with the fresh herbs and toss gently. Offer freshly grated Parmesan or Romano cheese for a garnish. Serve with a fresh green salad and warm, garlicky bread sticks.

Serves 4–5.

Garden Vegetable Linguini with Mint

A light and delectable pasta for a midsummer night's dreaming. The Mediterranean tastes of eggplant and red pepper are cooled with a creamy yogurt sauce, redolent with lemon and mint. This pasta is heavenly.

1 pound Italian linguini
2 tablespoons extra-virgin olive oil
1 onion, sliced into chunks
4–5 garlic cloves, minced
½ large red pepper, cored, seeded, sliced into chunks
1 cup eggplant, peeled, cubed
6 cremini or button mushrooms, sliced
¾ cup plain yogurt
1 cup shredded Parmesan cheese
Juice of half a lemon
½ cup chopped fresh mint
White pepper, freshly ground
Fresh mint leaves

Bring salted water to a rolling boil in a large pot and cook the pasta until al dente. Heat the olive oil in a skillet over medium heat and sauté the onion for 5 minutes. Add the garlic, red pepper, eggplant, and mushrooms and sauté 5–7 minutes, until the veggies are tender-crisp.

In a small nonstick saucepan (or double broiler), gently heat the yogurt and add in the Parmesan, stirring well. Sprinkle the lemon juice on the vegetables and toss in the mint. Add some freshly ground white pepper and season to taste.

When the pasta is done, drain and pour it into a warmed pasta serving bowl. Add the yogurt-Parmesan sauce and toss well. Cover the pasta with the sautéed vegetables and garnish with more mint.

Serves 4–5.

Summer Garden Couscous

Here is a light couscous fragrant with summer seasonings picked fresh from the Goddess' bounty.

2½–3 cups prepared
        Couscous, cooled

1½ cups diced roma
        tomatoes

1 cucumber, peeled,
        diced

3 tablespoons red onion,
        diced fine

½ yellow pepper, seeded,
        chopped

1 can chilled chickpeas,
        drained, rinsed

½ cup crumbled feta
        cheese

¼ cup water

3 tablespoons lemon
        juice

2 tablespoons extra-
        virgin olive oil

2 tablespoons chopped
        fresh mint

    Sea salt

    Black pepper, freshly
        ground

10 kalamata olives

    Sprigs of fresh mint

In a large mixing bowl, combine the prepared *Couscous* (Autumn, page 131) with the roma tomatoes, cucumber, onion, pepper, chickpeas, and feta. Combine the water, lemon juice, olive oil, and mint in a glass measuring cup and pour into the couscous mixture, tossing well to coat evenly. Add the kalamatas and stir. Garnish with sprigs of fresh mint.

Serve with *Spicy Hummus* (Autumn, page 105) for an easy, make-ahead light lunch. Offer fresh pita bread triangles and frosty iced tea with fresh mint sprigs to complete the meal.

Serves 4.

Couscous-Stuffed Zucchini

*What to do when friends and neighbors share their vegetable garden bounty with you . . .
and you have a dozen zucchini sitting in your refrigerator? Take some inspiration from
Eastern Mediterranean Goddesses and stuff your vegetables with sweetly spiced couscous.*

2	medium-large zucchini
2	tablespoons extra-virgin olive oil
1	red or yellow onion, diced
3–4	garlic cloves, minced
	Sea salt
	Black pepper, freshly ground
½	teaspoon cinnamon
½	teaspoon grated orange peel
⅓	cup couscous, uncooked
¾	cup vegetable broth or bouillon
2	tablespoons pine nuts, toasted
1–2	tablespoons golden raisins or chopped apricots

Preheat your oven to 375 degrees. Lightly oil a baking sheet. Wash the zucchini and trim the stems. Cut in half, lengthwise, and place the halves, cut side down, onto the baking sheet. Bake for 10–15 minutes. Remove from the oven and set aside to cool.

Reset your oven to 350 degrees. Using a spoon, carefully scoop out the center pulp of the zucchini, leaving a shell that is ¼-inch thick. Chop the pulp finely and set aside.

In a medium skillet, heat the olive oil over medium heat and sauté the onion for 5 minutes, until softened. Add in the garlic and chopped zucchini, sea salt, black pepper, cinnamon, and orange peel and stir for 1–2 minutes. Add in the couscous and stir to mix well.

Pour in the vegetable broth and bring to a high simmer. Cover and reduce heat to low. Gently simmer for 5 minutes. Uncover and remove from heat. Allow the stuffing to cool. Stir in the toasted pine nuts and golden raisins and mix well.

Place the zucchini shells in an oiled shallow baking dish and divide the filling between them, pressing in firmly. Cover with aluminum foil and bake in a 350-degree oven for about 20 minutes, until heated through.

Serve these stuffed zucchini hot or at room temperature with a summer salad and fresh pita bread.

Serves 4.

Southwestern Polenta

Corn symbolizes the life of the land and its cycles. Here is a sunny and spicy dish for celebrating the first harvest, perfect for a feast. In celebration of the Grain God, support your local brewers and purchase a fine assortment of ales, lagers, and stout. Offer red and white wines in honor of the grape harvest. Add some music and dancing and you may find Dionysus himself among your guests!

4	cups water
	Sea salt
1	cup stone-ground polenta cornmeal
1–2	tablespoons extra-virgin olive oil
1	onion, diced
1–2	jalapeño peppers, cored, seeded, sliced
1	small sweet pepper, cored, seeded, diced
4	garlic cloves, minced
1	teaspoon chili powder
1	can (14 ounces) diced tomatoes
1	cup *Basic Fresh Marinara Sauce* or good jarred sauce
2	tablespoons chopped fresh cilantro
¼	teaspoon fennel
2	cans (16 ounces each) black beans, drained, rinsed
4–6	ounces feta or chèvre goat cheese, sliced

Note: I have discovered a quick-cooking polenta, sold in bulk at my local health food market, that cooks up in 10 minutes and is absolutely delicious. It may be worth your while to investigate your local markets, especially if you adore polenta as much as I do. The cooking time that follows is for the original-style polenta.

Preheat your oven to 350 degrees. Pour the water into a saucepan and bring to a boil. Add a pinch of sea salt. Measure the cornmeal in a glass measuring cup and begin to pour the polenta into the boiling water, keeping a steady stream and stirring constantly as you pour. (I like to use a whisk to keep the lumps at a minimum.) Turn the heat down to low so as not to burn the polenta and keep stirring, smoothing out any lumps. Gently cook for 20 minutes, stirring regularly, keeping it smooth and creamy. The polenta is done when it begins to pull away from the sides of the pan.

Pour this cornmeal mush out onto a clean cutting board, mounding it into a long oval shape. Or, if you prefer, pour it into a shallow, oiled baking pan. Set aside to cool.

In a medium skillet, heat the olive oil and sauté the onions. Cook gently until onions begin to soften, about 5 minutes. Add the peppers, garlic, and chili

continued

powder, stir and sauté for 5–10 minutes. Add in the chopped tomatoes, *Basic Fresh Marinara Sauce* (Autumn, page 119), and herbs. Stir the ingredients together and remove from heat.

Set your oven to broil. Slice the cooled polenta loaf into pieces about 1-inch thick (or if you have cooled the polenta in a pan, you may cut it into triangles). Lay the slices in an oiled baking or broiling pan. Brush lightly with olive oil and gently broil the polenta until it browns at the edges. Remove the pan from the oven.

Layer your black beans over the broiled polenta slices. Next layer your tomato mixture. Top with the feta cheese slices. Bake at 350 degrees for 15–20 minutes, or until it is hot and bubbly.

Serves 4.

Vegetarian Goddess Tacos

A light, healthy taco brimming with fresh flavors and textures.

1–2 tablespoons extra-virgin olive oil
1 onion, thinly sliced
4 garlic cloves, minced
1 red pepper, cored, seeded, sliced very thin
2 Anaheim chili peppers, cored, seeded, chopped
1 teaspoon cumin
1 teaspoon chili powder
1 package baked seasoned Mexican-style tofu, sliced into bite-size pieces
2 tablespoons lime juice
1 tablespoon chopped fresh cilantro
   Sea salt
   Black pepper, freshly ground
8 corn tacos
16 cherry tomatoes, halved
2 cups shredded lettuce

In a large nonstick skillet, heat the olive oil over medium heat and sauté the onion and garlic for 3 minutes. Add the peppers, sprinkle with cumin and chili powder, and sauté until the peppers are tender-crisp, about 5 minutes. Add the baked tofu and sprinkle in lime juice and cilantro, mix together, and season with sea salt and freshly ground pepper, to taste. Remove from heat and set aside.

Set up the taco shells and fill each one halfway with the skillet mixture. Top with fresh shredded lettuce and tomatoes.

Note: If you do not have corn tacos, substitute with pita bread halves.

Serves 4.

Serving ideas

- Serve with a side dish of *Spanish Rice* (Autumn, page 135), *Green Goddess Guacamole* (Summer, page 53), and *Garlic Salsa* (Summer, page 54).

Vegetarian Burritos Deliciosos

I love the spices and flavors in Southwestern cooking, which seem to be infused with the colors and heat of the vibrant, southern sun itself.

6 large burrito-size tortillas

2½–3 cups cooked Texmati rice

1 can (1 pound) black beans, drained, rinsed

3 limes, quartered

2 tablespoons extra-virgin olive oil

1 Spanish onion, diced

½ red pepper, cored, seeded, diced

6 garlic cloves, minced

½ teaspoon chili powder

½ teaspoon cumin

6 ounces baked tofu, seasoned Mexican-style, sliced into bite-size strips

1 cup sweet corn, fresh or frozen (if frozen, thaw first)

Sea salt

Black pepper, freshly ground

¼ cup fresh chopped cilantro

1 avocado, peeled, pitted, sliced

Salsa (optional)

Light sour cream (optional)

Preheat your oven to 300 degrees. Wrap the tortillas in foil (or place in tortilla warmer) and heat in the oven for 10 minutes. Remove from the oven and set aside. In an ovenproof bowl or casserole dish, mix the rinsed black beans with the hot cooked rice, and squeeze half of the limes over the rice and beans. Stir well to mix. Cover and place in oven to heat through.

In a skillet, heat the olive oil over medium heat and sauté the onions until soft, about 5 minutes. Add the peppers and garlic, chili powder, and cumin and stir, cooking for about 5 minutes. Add in the sliced tofu, corn, sea salt, and black pepper. Stir and heat through, about 5 minutes. Add in the chopped cilantro and remove from heat.

Remove the rice mixture from the oven. Unwrap the warm tortillas and place one tortilla on a warmed plate. Spoon about ⅙ of the rice mixture, ⅙ of the vegetable/tofu mixture, and 2–3 slices of avocado across the center of the tortilla. Fold in the ends to cover the filling about 2 inches on each end, and roll/wrap the tortilla to form the burrito. Repeat for the other 5 tortillas.

Serve at once, with a fresh green salad on the side. Offer salsa, light sour cream, and remaining lime wedges as garnishes.

Serves 6.

Vegetable Stir-Fry in a Sweet and Savory Sauce

This quick and easy stir-fry is seasoned with an Asian-style sauce that is sweet and savory . . . a favorite Goddess combination. Serve this with steamed basmati rice and chopped cashews for garnish.

⅓ cup pineapple/orange juice (or peach/mango)

2 tablespoons low-sodium soy sauce

1 tablespoon molasses

1 inch fresh ginger, grated

½ teaspoon Chinese five-spice powder

3 garlic cloves, minced

2 tablespoons sesame oil

1 large onion, thinly sliced

3 carrots, sliced diagonally

1 cup small broccoli florets

1 cup cauliflower pieces

½ head white cabbage, shredded

1 red pepper, seeded, cored, julienned

1 cup pea pods, trimmed

1 can sliced water chestnuts, drained, rinsed

Basmati rice

Chopped cashews or peanuts

Combine the juice, soy sauce, molasses, spices, and garlic in a measuring cup and blend well. Set aside. In a large skillet, heat the oil over medium-high heat and quickly stir-fry the onion for 3 minutes.

Add the carrots, broccoli, cauliflower, cabbage, and pepper, stirring briskly for 5 minutes. Add in the pea pods and water chestnuts and stir-fry for 4–5 minutes. Add in the stir-fry sauce and mix well. Cook for another 3–5 minutes, until vegetables are just tender-crisp.

Serve over steamed basmati rice and garnish with chopped cashews or peanuts.

Serves 4.

Yellow Tomato and Portobello Mushroom Pizza

Sweet yellow tomatoes contrast earthy portobello mushrooms in this delightful summer pizza, sure to stir up a little appreciation. Every Goddess needs to feel appreciated.

2   tablespoons extra-
        virgin olive oil
1   large portobello
        mushroom,
        stemmed, sliced
6   garlic cloves, minced
        Pizza Dough,
        stretched and rolled
        out onto a pizza pan
2   medium yellow
        tomatoes, sliced
2   tablespoons sliced ripe
        black olives
½   cup fresh basil leaves,
        shredded
1   teaspoon marjoram,
        dried, or
        1 tablespoon fresh
4   ounces feta cheese,
        cubed
1   tablespoon extra-
        virgin olive oil

Preheat your oven to 400 degrees. In a medium skillet, heat the olive oil over medium heat and lightly sauté the mushroom slices and garlic for 2–3 minutes on each side. Set aside.

Drizzle the *Pizza Dough* (Spring, page 26) with a little olive oil and place the tomato slices around the pizza. Add the sautéed mushrooms and garlic along with the olives, basil, and marjoram. Finish with the cubes of feta cheese. Drizzle some olive oil over the tomatoes and around the edges of the crust.

Bake for 15–20 minutes, or until the crust is golden brown. Delicious enjoyed hot out of the oven or later at room temperature.

Serves 2–4.

Baked Eggplant with Goat Cheese

Honor the Greek Goddess Athena with this light, healthy version of traditional baked egg-plant. Add a plate of Athena's beloved olives, some fresh warm pita bread, a glass of wine . . . and you have a Goddess feast!

2 medium-size eggplants
  Extra-virgin olive oil
    or olive oil spray
1 cup (or more) Italian-
    style seasoned bread
    crumbs
6–8 roma tomatoes, sliced
4 garlic cloves, minced
2 tablespoons capers,
    rinsed
1 teaspoon marjoram
2 tablespoons chopped
    fresh Italian parsley
  Sea salt
  Black pepper, freshly
    ground
5 ounces chèvre goat
    cheese (or soy moz-
    zarella to keep it
    vegan)
1 tablespoon extra-
    virgin olive oil

Preheat your oven to 400 degrees. Slice the egg-plant ¼-inch thick. Brush lightly, or spray, with olive oil. Dip slices into a bowl of seasoned bread crumbs, arranging them on a baking sheet in a single layer. Bake for 10 minutes, until golden and slightly crisp.

Reset the oven temperature for 375 degrees. Oil a large baking dish and arrange the eggplant slices, overlapping if you need to. Cover the roasted egg-plant with the tomato slices and sprinkle with garlic, capers, marjoram, and parsley. Add a pinch of sea salt and freshly ground pepper and top with the goat cheese. Drizzle 1 tablespoon of extra-virgin olive oil lightly over the tomatoes and goat cheese, if desired.

Bake in a 375-degree oven for 15–20 minutes, until heated through and the cheese is melting.

Serve hot or at room temperature, along with a *Classic Greek Salad* (Summer, page 86) and a basket of hot, fresh sourdough rolls.

Serves 4.

Green Goddess Wraps

I created these sandwiches one day when I had run out of pita bread. They may easily be made up ahead of time and wrapped in plastic wrap or wax paper. Pack these along with some cold fresh lemonade and head out to a friendly shade tree, kick off your shoes, and relax into a lazy afternoon. It's good soul medicine.

4	large fresh flour tortillas (flavored tortillas are wonderful)
2	tablespoons sweet and hot mustard
2	cups baby spring greens salad mix
1	avocado, peeled, sliced (squeeze lemon juice on if not serving soon)
2	cups spicy sprouts
1	large carrot, peeled, shredded
1	large ripe red tomato, chopped
1–2	jalapeño peppers, sliced, or 1½ tablespoons jarred jalapeño slices
2–3	tablespoons chopped black olives
4	slices provolone-style soy cheese, cut into strips
3–4	tablespoons soy mayonnaise or egg mayonnaise

Lay out the tortillas and spread a little sweet hot mustard down the center. Divide all of the filling ingredients among the tortillas. Spoon over a little soy mayonnaise. Roll up the tortillas firmly, jelly-roll style.

If serving immediately, place on plate and secure with a toothpick, if desired. If packing for a picnic, wrap securely in wax paper.

Serves 4.

Savory Sides

Gingered Green Beans with Hazelnuts

Fresh summer green beans are such a treat. Here they are seasoned with a lovely combination of ginger, soy sauce, and crunchy hazelnuts.

2   tablespoons canola or sesame oil

4   garlic cloves, minced

2   inches fresh ginger, peeled and finely cut into thin sticks

Nutmeg

1   pound green beans, stemmed

1   tablespoon low-sodium soy sauce

1   tablespoon sesame oil

1   tablespoon dry sherry

½   teaspoon chili powder

Sea salt

Black pepper, freshly ground

2   tablespoons chopped hazelnuts

In a nonstick skillet, heat the oil over medium heat and sauté the garlic, ginger, and a pinch of nutmeg for about 1 minute. Add the green beans and stir for 1 minute.

In a measuring cup, combine the soy sauce, oil, sherry, chili powder, and seasonings and mix well. Pour over the green beans and lower the heat, cooking until the beans are tender-crisp. Toss in the chopped hazelnuts and serve immediately.

Note: If you do not have hazelnuts on hand, try cashews or almonds. We Goddesses should be flexible, you know. . . .

Serves 4.

Mediterranean Vegetable Sauté

A quick, light accompaniment to couscous or pasta. Throw this sauté together in 20 minutes, then let the dishes sit in the sink while you stroll outside to enjoy the summer evening until the fireflies come out.

3–4 tablespoons extra-
virgin olive oil
1 leek, sliced, white and
light green sections
only
4 garlic cloves, minced
1 medium eggplant,
peeled, cubed
1 cup broccoli florets
1 red pepper, seeded,
cored, julienned
2 carrots, peeled,
julienned
1 can (14 ounces)
artichoke hearts,
drained
1 cucumber, peeled,
julienned
12 kalamata or ripe black
olives
Juice of 1 lemon
¼ teaspoon fennel
Oregano
2 tablespoons chopped
fresh parsley
1 tablespoon chopped
fresh mint
Sea salt
Black pepper, freshly
ground

Heat the olive oil in a large skillet over medium heat and sauté the leeks and garlic for 3 minutes. Add the eggplant, broccoli, pepper, and carrots. Sauté 4–5 minutes, until tender-crisp. Add the artichokes, cucumber, and olives. Squeeze the lemon juice on, and add in the fennel and a good pinch of oregano. Season with sea salt and freshly ground pepper. Continue to sauté lightly 2–3 minutes. Serve when heated through.

Serving ideas
• Delicious warm with *Summer Garden Couscous* (Summer, page 66), or *Apricot Rice Pilaf* (Summer, page 82) and *Spicy Hummus* (Autumn, page 105).

Baked Three Beans with Pineapple

The mother of grain and crops, Demeter, is associated with beans as well. A summertime favorite, bring this dish along to any outdoor picnic in honor of Demeter's abundant season.

2 tablespoons canola oil

1 red onion, diced

1 can (1 pound) dark red kidney beans, drained, rinsed

1 can (1 pound) pinto beans, drained, rinsed

1 can (1 pound) black beans, drained, rinsed

1 can (8 ounces) chunk pineapple in natural juice

¼ cup molasses

¼ cup natural maple syrup

2 tablespoons tomato paste thinned with 2 tablespoons water

½ cup orange juice

1 tablespoon dry mustard

1 teaspoon Chinese five-spice powder

1 teaspoon curry powder

In a medium skillet, heat the oil and sauté the onions until softened. Combine all of the other ingredients in a mixing bowl and stir to mix well. When the onions are soft, stir them into the bean mixture. Pour the bean mixture into a baking crock or casserole and cover. Bake at 300 degrees for 1–1½ hours.

This is wonderful for serving at a backyard picnic. Hopefully there will be leftovers to enjoy the next morning at breakfast!

Serves 6.

Salsa Cruda

This is a classic fresh, uncooked tomato "sauce" to accompany Southwestern dishes. Include it with appetizers or toss it on hot pasta for a quick meal. Be creative!

8	ripe roma tomatoes, chopped
4	garlic cloves, minced
2	tablespoons extra-virgin olive oil
1½	tablespoons capers, rinsed
½	cup fresh shredded basil
2	tablespoons fresh chopped parsley
¼	cup fresh chopped cilantro
1	tablespoon lime juice
	Sea salt
	Black pepper, freshly ground

Combine all of the ingredients and enjoy.

Serving ideas

- Pair this with *Vegetarian Burritos Deliciosos* (Summer, page 71), *Black and White Enchiladas* (Winter, page 170), or even *Tofu Scramble* (Spring, page 31).

Corn Mother's Relish

This savory relish makes a perfect side dish for our earth mother's bounty.

5 tablespoons extra-virgin olive oil

3 tablespoons balsamic vinegar

¼ teaspoon cumin

2 tablespoons lime juice

Sea salt

¼ teaspoon red pepper flakes

4 ears of corn, kernels removed (about 2 cups)

1 sweet red pepper, seeded, diced

1 sweet green pepper, seeded, diced

4 roma tomatoes, halved, seeded

5 garlic cloves, minced

2 tablespoons extra-virgin olive oil

Sea salt

½ red onion, diced finely

1 can (1 pound) black beans, drained, rinsed

¼ cup fresh cilantro, chopped

2 tablespoons chopped fresh mint

Make the dressing by combining the olive oil, vinegar, cumin, lime juice, sea salt, and red pepper flakes in a small bowl.

Preheat your oven to 375 degrees. In an oiled roasting pan, combine the corn kernels, red and green peppers, roma tomatoes, and garlic. Drizzle with the extra-virgin olive oil and season with sea salt. Stir the vegetables to coat them well. Roast them in the oven for 15–20 minutes.

In a larger bowl, combine the diced red onion, black beans, cilantro, and mint.

Remove the roasted vegetables from the oven and set aside to cool. When cool enough to handle, lightly chop the tomatoes. Add them and the remaining roasted vegetables into the black bean mixture and stir well. Pour on the dressing and mix well. Chill in a covered container for 2 hours, or serve at room temperature.

Serves 6–8.

Serving ideas

- Try it with the *Baked Eggplant with Goat Cheese* (Summer, page 74) or *Vegetarian Goddess Tacos* (Summer, page 70).

Apricot Rice Pilaf

A summery twist to the classic rice pilaf, this fruity Vegetarian Goddess version goes superbly with fresh summer vegetables and crisp salad greens.

2 tablespoons extra-virgin olive oil

1 medium red onion, chopped

½ teaspoon ginger

1 cup basmati rice, uncooked

2 cups hot vegetable broth or bouillon

¼ cup slivered almonds or pine nuts

½ cup chopped dried apricots

Heat the oil in a saucepan over medium heat and sauté the onion and ginger for 5 minutes. Add in the uncooked rice and stir-fry 3–5 minutes. Pour in the hot vegetable broth and bring to a boil. Reduce heat to low, cover, and simmer for 20 minutes, until all the liquid is absorbed. Add the nuts and chopped apricots and mix together. Cover and heat through on low for 5 minutes.

Serves 4.

Serving ideas
- Serve with *Vegetable Stir-Fry in a Sweet and Savory Sauce* (Summer, page 72) or *Mediterranean Vegetable Sauté* (Summer, page 78) with *White Bean Hummus with Capers and Dill* (Winter, page 155).

Summer Salads

Savory Red Potato Salad

I actually prefer this potato salad slightly warm and make it just before I wish to serve it. You may also chill it, if you prefer, and serve it cool or close to room temperature. It's perfect full moon food.

12 small red potatoes, scrubbed, cut up
   Sea salt
   Black pepper, freshly ground
4   scallions, sliced
1   cup nonfat plain yogurt
2   teaspoons horseradish
2   teaspoons Dijon mustard
2   teaspoons dill
½   teaspoon caraway seeds (optional)
   Fresh dill sprigs

Bring a large pot of water to a boil and cook the potatoes about 12 minutes, until they are just fork-tender. Drain and pour them into a large serving bowl. Season with sea salt and freshly ground pepper, to taste, and add in the scallions.

In a mixing bowl, combine the yogurt, horseradish, mustard, dill, and caraway seeds and blend together to make a dressing. Pour this mixture over the warm potatoes and toss well to coat them evenly. Serve warm or cover and chill for later. Garnish with sprigs of fresh dill.

Serves 4–5.

Butterfly Pasta Salad

Make this eye-catching salad ahead of time in the cooler morning hours and chill it for an easy supper later on. Some Goddesses like to plan ahead.

½ pound Italian farfalle ("butterfly" pasta)

⅓ cup chopped red onion

2 cloves garlic, minced

¼ cup chopped yellow pepper

¼ cup chopped red pepper

1 cup halved ripe cherry tomatoes

3 tablespoons sliced black olives

2 tablespoons capers, rinsed

1 can (1 pound) chilled chickpeas, drained, rinsed

⅔ cup crumbled goat cheese or feta cheese

½ cup chopped fresh parsley

½ cup chopped fresh basil

½ teaspoon red pepper flakes

⅓ cup extra-virgin olive oil

2 tablespoons sherry or balsamic vinegar

2 tablespoons pine nuts

Bring a large pot of salted water to a rolling boil and cook the farfalle until al dente. Drain and rinse well with cold water. Drain again and pour into a large serving bowl.

In a medium mixing bowl, combine all of the other ingredients and toss with the pasta, mixing gently. Cover and chill to let the flavors mingle, or serve at room temperature immediately if you simply can't wait!

Serves 4–5.

Spaghetti Salad with Tofu and Olives

A Vegetarian Goddess pasta salad accented with cooling Mediterranean flavors. Fish-eating Goddesses can substitute tuna or salmon for the tofu, if desired.

½ cup extra-virgin olive oil

½ cup chopped fresh Italian parsley

½ cup chopped fresh basil

4 garlic cloves, minced

2 tablespoons capers, rinsed, drained

12 kalamata olives

3 green onions, sliced diagonally

½ cup roasted red pepper, chopped

1 package baked seasoned tofu, sliced into bite-size pieces

3 tablespoons balsamic vinegar

1 tablespoon lemon juice

¼ teaspoon red chili flakes

Sea salt

Black pepper, freshly ground

1 pound spaghetti, broken in half

Feta cheese

Fresh parsley, chopped

Combine the olive oil, herbs, garlic, capers, olives, green onions, roasted peppers, tofu, vinegar, lemon juice, and spices in a large serving bowl. Cover and let marinate at room temperature for 30 minutes, to give the flavors time to develop.

Boil a large pot of salted water and cook the spaghetti until al dente. Drain and rinse in cold water. Drain again. Toss the room-temperature pasta with the marinade and mix well. Garnish with crumbled feta cheese or fresh chopped parsley.

Serve at room temperature immediately or cover and chill.

Serves 4–6.

Classic Greek Salad

Every Athena knows that there are days when it's simply too hot to cook. Pick up some bakery fresh bread and hard boil a few eggs to round out this classic salad into a light meal.

6	cups mixed salad greens
1	cucumber, skinned, sliced
½	red onion, sliced
12–16	cherry tomatoes
12–16	kalamata olives
8	pepperoncini, drained
4	ounces crumbled feta cheese

Greek Dressing

2	tablespoons extra-virgin olive oil
2	tablespoons wine or sherry vinegar
1	teaspoon Greek oregano
2	garlic cloves, minced
	Sea salt
	Black pepper, freshly ground

Combine the greens, cucumber, onion, tomatoes, olives, pepperoncini, and feta in a chilled bowl. Make the *Greek Dressing* (below) and pour over the greens just before serving. Serve on cold plates with chilled, sliced hard-boiled eggs for added protein.

Serves 4–6.

Greek Dressing

Whisk together the oil, vinegar, oregano, garlic, and seasonings and dress the salad.

Eastern Goddess Summer Salad

I first had an Asian salad at my sister's house, when she and her husband were married in an intimate alfresco ceremony. Part of the lovely buffet was a salad of mixed greens dressed in intriguing Asian flavors of ginger and soy sauce. Here is my version, inspired by her wedding day salad.

2–3	cups baby spinach leaves, washed
2	cups mesclun greens, washed
1	cup bean sprouts, washed
1	cup sliced mushrooms
½	chilled red onion, sliced thinly
½	cup chilled mandarin orange slices
1	can (8 ounces) chilled, sliced water chestnuts, drained, rinsed
½	cup cashew pieces

Ginger Dressing

3	tablespoons sesame oil
3	tablespoons sherry vinegar or rice vinegar
3	tablespoons low-sodium soy sauce or tamari sauce
1	inch fresh ginger, grated
1	garlic clove, minced
½	teaspoon sugar
¼	teaspoon white pepper, freshly ground

Combine all of the salad ingredients in a large chilled bowl. Make the *Ginger Dressing* (below). Pour over the crisp salad greens right before serving, tossing well. Serve on chilled glass plates.

Serves 4–6.

Ginger Dressing

Combine all of the dressing ingredients and dress the salad.

Curried Slaw

This mildly spicy and sweet summer slaw is a cooling side dish to any favorite warm weather fare.

3 cups thinly shredded white cabbage
3 cups thinly shredded red cabbage
1 cup nonfat plain yogurt
3 tablespoons orange juice
1 teaspoon orange zest
1 tablespoon sherry vinegar
1 teaspoon honey mustard
2 garlic cloves, minced
1 teaspoon curry powder
½ teaspoon ginger
¼ cup toasted cashew pieces

In a large bowl, combine the shredded cabbages. In a small mixing bowl, make the dressing by combining the yogurt, orange juice, zest, vinegar, mustard, garlic, and spices. Whisk together well. Pour over the shredded cabbage and toss well to coat. Cover and chill for 2 hours. Add in the cashews just before serving to keep them crisp. Serve chilled.

Serves 8–10.

Fresh Summer Greens and Grapes in a Basil-Citrus Vinaigrette

Try this lively combination of citrus and fresh basil for a refreshing accent to your spicy Lughnasadh feast.

2   tablespoons extra-virgin olive oil

1   tablespoon orange juice

1   tablespoon sherry vinegar

1   teaspoon grated lemon zest

2   tablespoons chopped fresh basil

Sea salt

Black pepper, freshly ground

Assorted fresh greens, chilled

Grapes, chilled

Combine the olive oil, juice, vinegar, zest, basil, and seasonings. Dress your chilled summer greens and grapes just before serving.

Sweet Endings

Cappuccino Ice Cream

One of my husband Steve's favorite things in life is a good cappuccino. He is the designated cappuccino maker in the family, and we will often enjoy one together after dinner. In the heat of the summer, however, a frozen dessert with the cappuccino flavors of espresso and cinnamon is a cooler alternative.

⅔ cup chilled strong espresso (decaf is fine)

1½ cups milk or vanilla-almond milk

½ cup half-and-half or soy cream

1 cup sugar

1 teaspoon vanilla extract

¼ teaspoon cinnamon

Nutmeg

¼ teaspoon xanthan gum (optional)

Combine the chilled espresso, milk, half-and-half, and sugar in a blender. Cover and whip until the sugar is dissolved. Add the vanilla, cinnamon, pinch of nutmeg, and xanthan gum. Whip until smooth and frothy. Pour into an ice cream maker and freeze according to manufacturer's instructions.

Serve in festive dessert glasses with an extra sprinkling of nutmeg or cinnamon on top.

Serves 4–5.

Fried Bananas with Cashews

A popular way to enjoy bananas in the Southwest, frying up this simple fruit brings out its natural sweetness even more. Top it with a scoop of vanilla ice cream if you so desire.

2 tablespoons canola oil
3–4 ripe bananas, peeled, sliced diagonally
    Cinnamon
4 tablespoons chopped cashews

Heat the oil in a nonstick skillet over medium heat and gently sauté the bananas. Sprinkle with a dash of cinnamon and cook until the bananas are soft and starting to brown at the edges. Sprinkle with the cashew pieces at the last minute and serve on dessert plates.

Serves 3–4 (plan on one banana per person).

Orange Sherbet with Chocolate Chips

Orange is love and fidelity, and we all know that chocolate is love . . . that makes this dessert the perfect choice in celebrating a Goddess Midsummer festival!

1½ cups orange juice

1 cup sugar

1 teaspoon grated orange zest

1 teaspoon natural orange extract

1 cup (unsweetened) coconut milk

¼ teaspoon xanthan gum (optional)

½ cup mini semisweet chocolate chips

In a blender, combine the orange juice, sugar, orange zest, and extract. Cover and whip until the sugar is dissolved. Add the coconut milk and xanthan gum. Whip until it is smooth and frothy, about 3–5 minutes. Pour into an ice cream maker and stir in the mini chocolate chips. Freeze according to manufacturer's instructions. Pass out the spoons and kisses.

Serves 4–5.

Lavender Cookies

The summer solstice brings us the first harvest of lavender buds. Bake up some love magick in your oven early in the morning before the day gets too hot. Makes a classic summer combination with sherbet.

2   sticks unsalted butter or margarine, room temperature
1   cup superfine sugar
½   teaspoon sea salt
2   free-range eggs, well beaten
2   teaspoons vanilla extract
1   teaspoon lavender buds
2½ cups unbleached all-purpose flour

In a large bowl, cream the butter, sugar, and salt until fluffy. Add the beaten eggs and vanilla. Mix well. Add in the flour and mix on low speed just until the dough is coming together. Sprinkle in the lavender buds and fold in gently (don't overmix).

Divide the dough into two mounds and wrap up well in plastic. Chill in the refrigerator for one hour at least.

Preheat oven to 375 degrees. Flour your work surface and unwrap the dough. Take half of it out and wrap up the other half to keep chilled in the fridge while you work. Roll out the dough with a floured rolling pin, taking care not to overwork or overstretch the tender dough.

Cut out shapes of hearts, full moons, stars, and crescents. Carefully move the cookie shapes to nonstick cookie sheets, placing them ½-inch apart, fitting as many as possible on each sheet.

Bake, two sheets at a time, until the cookies are golden brown, about 6–8 minutes. Use a thin spatula to move the hot cookies to a rack to cool. Store in an airtight container when cooled.

Serve with some *Orange Sherbet with Chocolate Chips* (Summer, page 93).

Makes about 3 dozen.

Serving idea

• Serve in the afternoon with cold, fresh lemonade or iced tea with mint sprigs.

Amen Farm Apple Cake

One of my oldest and dearest friends contributed this old-fashioned recipe for apple cake. Martha is an Equestrian Goddess who loves horses and farm life, and creates beauty everyday with her home and family.

3 cups unbleached all-purpose flour

1 cup white sugar

1 cup brown sugar

1 teaspoon baking soda

½ teaspoon sea salt

2 teaspoons cinnamon

½ teaspoon nutmeg

3 free-range eggs or egg substitute

1 cup canola oil

½ cup plain yogurt

2 teaspoons vanilla

3 cups chopped, peeled apples (assorted is nice, choose 2 or 3 varieties)

1 cup walnuts (optional)

Preheat your oven to 350 degrees. Lightly grease and flour a bundt pan or a 9 by 13-inch cake pan. In a large mixing bowl, mix the dry ingredients together. Add in the eggs, oil, yogurt, and vanilla. Beat until smooth.

Fold in the chopped apples and walnuts. Pour the batter into the pan and bake for about 1 hour in a bundt pan; 40–45 minutes in a rectangular pan. Cool on wire rack.

Turn the cake out onto a serving plate. Serve with your favorite mugs of steaming coffee and a good story or two.

Serves 6–8.

Classic Key Lime Pie

What Goddess can resist the tart sweetness in this enchanting summer dessert? Using a prepared graham cracker pie crust makes this tempting treat a simple task.

3   large free-range egg yolks, beaten

1   can (15 ounces) sweetened condensed milk

¾   cup lime juice, freshly squeezed

3   teaspoons grated lime zest

9   inch prepared graham cracker pie crust

¾   cup whipping cream, well chilled

¼   cup superfine sugar or powdered sugar

Lime zest strips

Preheat your oven to 325 degrees. Briskly whisk together the beaten egg yolks, condensed milk, and fresh lime juice until it is frothy. Add in the grated zest and beat until the filling is smooth. Pour the filling into the graham cracker pie shell.

Bake the pie in the center of your oven for about 15 minutes or so, until the filling is set, but still quivers slightly. Set the pie on a rack to cool completely, then cover and chill in the refrigerator.

When you are ready to serve, whip the chilled cream with the sugar until it forms stiff peaks. Serve each wedge of chilled pie on a cold dessert plate and top with a generous dollop of whipped cream. Decorate each piece with a curled strip of lime zest, if desired.

Serves 6–8.

Notes on your favorite Summer recipes

As the Wheel of the Year turns to autumn, the Goddess has welcomed the harvest and given freely of her summer **bounty**. As Demeter, Mother of Grain and cultivated crops, she rests now after her labor. The full Harvest Moon circles across the sky and becomes the Blood Moon, or **Pumpkin** Moon. The Goddess moves a little slower in the shorter days of fall, transitioning into her Crone aspect, anticipating the **colder** nights ahead.

As Hecate, and Kali, she is **wise** woman and priestess. She beckons for us to let go of the **past**, the old and outdated parts of our lives that no longer serve us. She urges us to prepare for our night **journey** that surely lies ahead. The Goddess now stands in the west, at home with the thunderbeings and dark waters. For water is her element. She is **familiar** with sorrow. Her robe is black. And each silver strand of hair bespeaks of her hard-won wisdom. It is time to prepare for **introspection**, and savor the bittersweet joys that autumn brings to us.

Autumn

Festival Menus

Autumn Equinox (aka Mabon)

Around September 21, the balance of light and dark occurs again, this time with the dark hours beginning their gain. We celebrate the second harvest, knowing that the colder days of winter are not far off. It is a time for enjoying the fruits of our labors, a time for feasting and thanksgiving. The Great Goddess has been good to us. Gather the last of your herbs and hang them for drying. Fill your home with fruits of the season—pumpkins, gourds, and corn. Light candles of yellow, orange, and purple to honor health, sharing the harvest, and a deepening spiritual awareness. Burn rosemary for protection and longevity. Plan for a time of study and begin looking through some new books to ignite your interest.

Harvest Sangria *(page 103)*

Spicy Hummus *(page 105)*

Cinnamon Cornbread *(page 108)*

Piquant Corn and Tomato Chowder *(page 112)*

Tri-Colored Stuffed Peppers *(page 120)*

Salad Greens and Oranges with Raspberry Vinaigrette *(page 140)*

Bread Pudding *(page 146)*

Hallow's Eve (aka Samhain)

Legend tells us that at the night of Samhain, the veil between two worlds is the thinnest and spirits may pass between. South American cultures celebrate this as the Day of the Dead. For followers of the Goddess, October 31 is the eve of the Celtic New Year, a time for the Goddess to step fully into her Crone aspect as winter herself. As Rhiannon, Queen of the Night, the Goddess is the shapeshifter, often seen as an elegant stag, regal with power and strength, surrendering to instinctual energies. Her lesson is: follow your instincts.

Wear patchouli oil for grounding and light candles for illumination. Burn sage and cedar to cleanse negativity and purify your energy. Look ahead with peace in your heart, and renew your commitment to the earth, to the Goddess, knowing that she is eternal.

Mulled Cider *(page 104)*
Savory Hot Artichoke Spread *(page 106)*
Rosemary Cheese Biscuits *(page 109)*
Roasted Acorn Squash Risotto *(page 122)*
Apple Cranberry Crisp *(page 143)*

Beverages and Bites

Harvest Sangria

Make this fruity, thirst-quenching classic a few hours ahead, to allow all of the flavors to develop. Then let the celebration begin!

2 bottles full-bodied red wine

1 can frozen cranberry juice concentrate

2 tablespoons lemon juice

¾ cup Triple Sec

¼ cup sugar

1 orange, washed, sliced in rounds

1 lime, washed, sliced

1 lemon, washed, sliced

1 pear, washed, sliced

1 apple, washed, sliced

1 bottle chilled lemon-lime seltzer

Cracked ice

Combine everything but the flavored seltzer and ice in a large container. Stir, cover, and chill for a few hours.

In a large pitcher or punch bowl, combine the wine mixture with the lemon-lime seltzer and some cracked ice. Let the music begin. . . .

Mulled Cider

Apples are earth magick, and nothing compares to the seasonal treat of fresh apple cider. So brew up some of the Goddess' favorite magick with apples for love and health, cinnamon for luck and money, and cloves for protection.

1   quart fresh apple cider
     Juice of 1 orange
1   orange, washed and
        sliced in rounds
1   apple, washed, sliced
        horizontally, to
        reveal the center star
     Whole cloves
3   cinnamon sticks

Pour the cider into a soup pot (or slow cooker, if you have the time to heat it slowly) and squeeze in the orange juice. Add the orange slices. Stud each round apple slice with 5 whole cloves. Gently add them to the cider and toss in the cinnamon sticks. Heat the cider on low heat for at least 15 minutes before serving.

Serves 6–8.

Spicy Hummus

A spicier version of the classic hummus, serve with toasted pita chips as an appetizer with the harvest sangria.

1 can (1 pound) chick-
    peas, drained, rinsed
1–2 tablespoons extra-
    virgin olive oil
⅛ cup vegetable broth
    or water
4 garlic cloves, crushed
¼ cup natural peanut
    butter
1 tablespoon finely
    chopped red onion
1 jalapeño or chili
    pepper, seeded,
    finely chopped
    Juice of 1 lime
¼ teaspoon curry powder
¼ teaspoon chili powder
    Cayenne pepper
    Sea salt
    White pepper, freshly
    ground
2 scallions, chopped
    (optional)

Toasted Pita Chips
8 pita breads
    Olive oil spray
    Parmesan cheese,
    grated (optional)

Place the chickpeas, olive oil, broth, garlic, peanut butter, onion, jalapeno, lime juice, curry, chili powder, and a pinch of cayenne pepper into a blender or food processor. Cover and purée the hummus, until it is a creamy consistency. Taste for seasoning adjustments, adding more lime juice or spices as desired. Garnish with chopped scallions.

Serve as an appetizer with *Toasted Pita Chips* (below) and fresh crisp carrot sticks.

Serves 6–8.

Serving idea

- Use as a side dish with roasted vegetables and couscous. *Serves 4–6.*

Toasted Pita Chips

Preheat your oven to 400 degrees. Slice the pita breads into triangular pieces and place on an oiled baking sheet. Spray with olive oil and sprinkle with Parmesan, if desired. Bake for 10 minutes or until the triangles are browned and crispy.

Serves 4 (plan on 2 pita breads per person).

Savory Hot Artichoke Spread

Spiked with green chilies and pine nuts, this melting hot spread is delicious on Toasted Pita Chips or your favorite cracker.

1   can (14 ounces)
     artichoke hearts,
     drained, chopped
⅔   cup soy mayonnaise
½   cup grated Parmesan
     cheese
4   ounces green chilies,
     drained, chopped
1   teaspoon curry powder
⅛   teaspoon cumin
     Black pepper, freshly
     ground
⅓   cup pine nuts, lightly
     toasted
2   tablespoons grated
     Parmesan or Asiago
     cheese

Preheat your oven to 350 degrees. In a small bowl, mash the artichoke hearts and mix in the soy mayonnaise. Add in the Parmesan, green chilies, spices, and pine nuts. Blend with a fork.

Place the spread in an ovenproof serving dish and top with 2 tablespoons of Parmesan. Bake for 20 minutes, until heated through.

Serve at once with *Toasted Pita Chips* (Autumn, page 105) or crackers.

Serves 4–6.

Focaccia Baked with Jalapeños and Feta

There is nothing quite like the warm and earthy texture of a freshly baked focaccia, a favorite of Italian Goddesses. Here I have combined spicy jalapeños with tangy feta cheese, creating a bread that has a satisfying, lively character.

1½	teaspoons dry active yeast
3	cups unbleached flour
1	tablespoon cornmeal
1	teaspoon sea salt
1	tablespoon honey
3	tablespoons extra-virgin olive oil
1¼	cups warm water
1	tablespoon dried cilantro or parsley
1	teaspoon red pepper flakes
4	garlic cloves, minced
¼	cup crumbled feta cheese
2	tablespoons coarsely chopped jalapeño pepper

Bread machine: Combine all of the ingredients in the order that your particular manufacturer recommends. Set the cycle for "dough" and "large loaf."

By hand: Please follow the same instructions listed for *Sun-Dried Tomato Focaccia* (Spring, pages 12–13) to create the dough.

When the dough has risen, turn it out onto a baking sheet dusted with cornmeal, and flatten it with floured fingers, or a rolling pin, into a 12 to 14-inch oval or circle. (If you are using a pizza stone, turn out the dough onto a floured peel.) Brush the surface with olive oil and cover with a clean towel. Set aside to rise for 20 minutes, until doubled in height.

Preheat your oven to 400 degrees. (If you are using a pizza stone, warm it in the oven while the dough is rising.) When the dough has risen, use your finger to dimple the surface all over and sprinkle with coarse salt. Place the focaccia in the upper half of your oven and bake at 400 degrees for 10 minutes.

Lower the oven temperature to 350 degrees and continue baking for another 12 minutes or so, until the bread is golden brown. Cool on a wire rack.

Serve warm, sliced into wedges, or later at room temperature.

Serves 6–8.

Cinnamon Cornbread

The sweet warmth of cinnamon pairs beautifully with the cornmeal here for a light, grainy accompaniment to any spicy meal.

¼ cup canola oil

1¼ cups stone-ground cornmeal

¾ cup unbleached all-purpose flour

1 teaspoon baking soda

1½ teaspoons baking powder

¼ teaspoon sea salt

3 tablespoons sugar

2 free-range eggs, beaten

1 cup milk

1 teaspoon cinnamon

½ teaspoon allspice

⅛ teaspoon ground cloves

Preheat your oven to 400 degrees. Oil a 9 by 9-inch baking pan. Combine all of the ingredients in a mixing bowl and blend, keeping it a bit lumpy. Pour the batter into the prepared baking pan and sprinkle some extra cinnamon over the top, swirling it into the batter slightly.

Bake for 20–25 minutes, until done. The center should spring back when touched. Let it sit 5–10 minutes before cutting, if you can resist.

Serves 4–6.

Rosemary Cheese Biscuits

Old-fashioned biscuits are a treat in any season. According to Goddess lore, sprinkling rosemary into the dough helps us to attract love and longevity. Rosemary also means remembrance, making it appropriate for the night of Samhain.

2 cups unbleached all-purpose flour

½ cup grated Parmesan cheese

2½ teaspoons baking powder

¼ teaspoon sea salt

1 teaspoon fresh rosemary, minced

Cayenne pepper

1 stick unsalted butter or margarine, chilled

½ cup milk

2 teaspoons dry sherry

Preheat oven to 425 degrees. In a large bowl, combine the flour, Parmesan, baking powder, salt, rosemary, and a pinch of cayenne. Cut the chilled butter into pieces and mix into the flour mixture, crumbling the dough. Add the milk and dry sherry and quickly mix the dough, just until the ingredients are barely moistened. This keeps the dough tender.

Form the dough into a ball and place on a floured surface. Roll out the dough with floured fingers (or a floured rolling pin) to about ½-inch thick. Cut out rounds with a cookie cutter or jelly glass and place them on a baking sheet.

Bake for 10–12 minutes, until they are golden brown. Serve warm in a festive basket.

Makes about 18 biscuits.

Seasonal Soups

Tortellini Supper Soup

This recipe came about one afternoon when I was searching for the ingredients to make a vegetable soup and felt that something was missing. Taking inspiration from the Italian Goddesses, I added tortellini. Bravo!

2	tablespoons extra-virgin olive oil
1	medium onion, diced
5	garlic cloves, minced
2	carrots, scrubbed, chopped
5½	cups vegetable broth
1	can (28 ounces) crushed tomatoes
1	teaspoon sugar
1	cup cut green beans
1	tablespoon balsamic vinegar
	Sea salt
	Black pepper, freshly ground
½	pound cheese-filled (or spinach) tortellini
1	medium zucchini, sliced, quartered
1	teaspoon dried basil
1	teaspoon marjoram
¼	cup fresh chopped Italian parsley
	Parmesan cheese, shredded

In a heavy soup pot, heat the olive oil over medium heat and sauté the onions for 5 minutes. Add the garlic and carrots and stir-fry 3 minutes. Add the broth, tomatoes, sugar, green beans, balsamic vinegar, salt, and pepper. Heat to a boil, add the tortellini, and simmer for 15 minutes.

Add the zucchini and dried herbs and simmer for 10 minutes, until the zucchini is tender and the tortellini is done. Add in the chopped fresh parsley.

Serve immediately with a serving bowl of shredded Parmesan and some warm, garlicky bread sticks.

Serves 4–6.

Piquant Corn and Tomato Chowder

The sweet and spicy flavor of curry and the smoky heat of chipotle add a savory twist to this corn chowder. Take advantage of the late summer's harvest and use fresh corn and the last of the ripe summer tomatoes, if you are able.

2 tablespoons extra-virgin olive oil

1 medium Spanish onion, diced

1 celery stalk, chopped

1 teaspoon cumin

2 teaspoons curry powder

½–1 teaspoon mild chili powder

2 cups vegetable broth

1 can (28 ounces) cut plum tomatoes

2 tablespoons chopped fresh cilantro

2–3 cups sweet corn kernels

Ground chipotle

Sea salt

White pepper, freshly ground

3 cups milk or nondairy milk

Fresh cilantro, chopped

In a heavy soup pot, heat the olive oil over medium heat and sauté the onion and celery for 5 minutes. Stir in the spices and cook for 3 minutes. Add the broth, tomatoes, and cilantro and bring to a boil. Reduce heat and simmer 10 minutes.

Add the sweet corn and season with a pinch of chipotle, sea salt, and pepper, to taste. Bring to a simmer over low heat, gently cooking until the corn is tender, about 10–15 minutes. Add in the milk and warm through gently. Taste for seasoning adjustments.

Serve immediately with a garnish of chopped cilantro and a basket of fresh warm tortillas.

Serves 4.

Autumn Warming Soup

When the days are getting shorter and the light more golden, nothing nourishes the body and spirit more than a pot of homemade soup simmering in the kitchen. Make a warming supper of this immune-boosting soup and a hearty loaf of peasant-style bread.

2	tablespoons extra-virgin olive oil
1	medium red onion, diced
½	head white cabbage, thinly shredded
6–7	carrots, scrubbed, cut into coins
4–5	garlic cloves, minced
1	teaspoon red pepper flakes
1	inch fresh ginger, grated, or 1 teaspoon ground ginger
1	teaspoon curry powder Black pepper, freshly ground
5	cups vegetable broth
1	cup fresh water
1	zucchini, quartered
6–8	small red potatoes, scrubbed, cut into bite-size pieces
1	sweet potato, peeled, diced
1	package (4 ounces) fresh shiitake mushrooms, sliced
1	cup frozen baby peas
2	teaspoons Italian herbs
1	can (14½ ounces) chopped tomatoes
¼	cup dry sherry

In a heavy soup pot, heat the olive oil over medium heat and sauté the onion until translucent. Add the cabbage, carrots, garlic, and spices. Stir, cooking for about 10 minutes.

When the vegetables are tender-crisp, add in the broth, water, zucchini, potatoes, mushrooms, peas, herbs, and tomatoes. Stir in the dry sherry.

Heat through on medium-high heat until simmering, then lower the heat and gently simmer for 45–50 minutes, until the vegetables are fork-tender.

Serve with warm rolls or a crusty bread.

Serves 4–6.

Golden Potato Soup

On a particularly cold November afternoon, my husband brought home a paper sack filled with Yellow Finn potatoes. Smallish, firm, and gold in color, they inspired me to pair them with parsnip and sweet potato. The result was this velvety, golden soup.

2　tablespoons extra-virgin olive oil

1　yellow onion, diced

1　celery stalk, chopped

5　garlic cloves, crushed

½　teaspoon curry powder

5　carrots, scrubbed, chopped

1　medium parsnip, peeled, chopped

4　cups vegetable broth

1　cup fresh water

8　Yellow Finn potatoes, peeled, cut up (or any gold potatoes)

½　large sweet potato, peeled, diced

¼　cup dry sherry

　　Sea salt

　　White pepper, freshly ground

¾　cup milk or nondairy milk

　　Nutmeg

In a heavy soup pot, heat the olive oil over medium heat and sauté the onion for 3 minutes. Add the celery and garlic, stirring for 2 minutes. Add the curry powder, carrots, and parsnip, stirring to coat. When the onions are browned, add the broth and water, all the potatoes, sherry, sea salt, and white pepper. Simmer the potatoes for 20–30 minutes, until they are fork-tender.

Carefully ladle half of the soup mixture into a blender. Cover and purée for 2–3 minutes. Add ½ cup milk and blend. Add the rest of the soup to the blender and purée with enough milk to make the soup smooth and creamy. Return the puréed soup to the soup pot and gently heat through, taking care not to boil. Add in the nutmeg. Taste and adjust the seasonings.

Serve piping hot with big slices of crusty bread and a dish of extra-virgin olive oil for dipping.

Serves 4–6.

Spicy Vegetarian Chili

While the frost faeries are busy with their icy magick, spice up some grounding earth energy for your family with this perennial favorite. (This recipe can easily be converted to an all-day simmer in a slow cooker. Simply combine all the ingredients raw, with no pre-cooking, and set the temperature on low. The chili should be ready in about 5–6 hours.)

1–2	tablespoons extra-virgin olive oil
1	large red onion, diced
1	sweet red pepper, cored, seeded, diced
1	can (28 ounces) chopped tomatoes with juice
5–6	garlic cloves, minced
1	bottle favorite chili sauce
½	cup molasses
½	cup fresh water (or more to thin)
1	tablespoon good chili powder
2	teaspoons ginger
2	teaspoons curry powder
1–2	teaspoons red pepper flakes
2	cans (1 pound each) dark red kidney beans, drained, rinsed
1	can (1 pound) black beans, drained, rinsed
1	can (1 pound) pinto or chili beans, drained, rinsed

In a heavy pot, heat the olive oil over medium high heat and sauté the onion and red pepper, until softened. Add the large can of tomatoes, garlic, chili sauce, molasses, and water. Stir together and add the spices.

Gently add in the beans, stirring with a wooden spoon. Bring to a high simmer, then lower the heat and let the chili simmer slowly. (This recipe can be ready to eat in as little as an hour, but I think that the longer it simmers, the better the flavor.)

This chili is wonderful served on a bed of steamed basmati rice, or simply ladled into chili bowls and topped with a dollop of light sour cream.

Serves 6.

Serving idea

- A basket of warm *Cinnamon Cornbread* (Autumn, page 108) is always the perfect addition.

Harvest Moon Soup

Celebrate the Harvest Moon with this magickal soup, crafted from the moon vegetables of cauliflower and potatoes. Creamy and satisfying.

2 tablespoons canola oil

1 yellow onion, diced

2 carrots, scrubbed, chopped

1 large celery stalk, chopped fine

½ teaspoon fennel

1–2 teaspoons curry powder

3 medium Yukon Gold potatoes, peeled, cut up

½ head cauliflower, cored, chopped into bite-size pieces

Sea salt

White pepper, freshly ground

Fresh water

1 can (14 ounces) coconut milk

In a heavy soup pot, heat the olive oil over medium heat and sauté the onion, until soft. Add the carrots, celery, and spices and stir, cooking for 2 minutes. Add in the potatoes, cauliflower, sea salt, white pepper, and enough fresh water to cover the vegetables completely. Bring to a boil, lower the heat, and simmer for 1 hour. Check the water level from time to time, making sure that the vegetables are always covered. Add a little water if necessary.

When the vegetables are tender, ladle the soup into a blender, reserving about a cup of the vegetable pieces in the soup pot. Cover the blender and purée the soup for 3–4 minutes, until it is smooth and creamy. Add the purée back into the pot with the vegetable pieces, stir in the coconut milk, and heat through on low heat for another 10–15 minutes.

Serve in bowls with a basket of muffins and a plate of salad greens in *Ginger Dressing* (Summer, page 87).

Serves 4.

Everyday Feasts

East Meets West Pasta

The following recipe takes a European pasta and infuses it with Eastern flavors, creating an exotic blend of East and West. Don't we Goddesses just love to mix things up?

1 pound Italian linguini or spaghetti
2 tablespoons sesame oil
1 cup white cabbage, finely shredded
6 garlic cloves, minced
1 cup broccoli florets
3 carrots, peeled, julienned
1–2 inches of fresh ginger, grated
1 teaspoon red pepper flakes
1 cup shiitake mushrooms, stemmed, sliced
1 can (8 ounces) sliced water chestnuts, drained
¼ cup vegetable broth or bouillon
1 tablespoon dry sherry
4 tablespoons low-sodium soy or tamari sauce
1 tablespoon rice or sherry vinegar
4 scallions, sliced diagonally
Sesame seeds

Bring a large pot of salted water to a rolling boil and cook the pasta until al dente. Heat the sesame oil over medium-high heat in a large skillet. Toss in the cabbage, garlic, broccoli, and carrots and stir-fry for about 5 minutes. Add in the ginger, red pepper flakes, mushrooms, and water chestnuts. Continue to stir-fry.

Combine the broth, sherry, soy sauce, and vinegar in a measuring cup. When the vegetables are tender-crisp, pour in the sauce, toss in the scallions, and mix.

When the pasta is ready, drain and pour into a warmed serving bowl. Add the vegetable sauce, and toss well. Sprinkle with sesame seeds, if desired.

Serve immediately in warmed, large bowls and offer a mixed green salad topped with mandarin oranges and bean sprouts in a *Raspberry Vinaigrette* (Autumn, page 140).

Serves 4–6.

Roasted Vegetable Lasagna

Melting goat cheese and roasted vegetables nestled into a layered lasagna dish makes any dinner a feast. This is a bountiful dish.

9–10	lasagna noodles, cooked, drained
1	large onion, chopped
1	sweet red pepper, cored, seeded, chopped
1	cup broccoli florets, cut into bite-size pieces
1	small eggplant, peeled, cubed
1	cup sliced cremini or chopped portobello mushrooms
5–6	roma tomatoes, quartered
8	garlic cloves, sliced
2	tablespoons extra-virgin olive oil
½	tablespoon dried marjoram
½	teaspoon thyme
½	teaspoon oregano
½	tablespoon dried basil
	Sea salt
	Black pepper, freshly ground
1	can (16 ounces) black or northern white beans, drained, rinsed
1	can (14 ounces) artichoke hearts, drained, sliced
4	cups *Basic Fresh Marinara Sauce*
8–10	ounces goat cheese

Preheat oven to 350 degrees. Drizzle a little olive oil over the cooked lasagna noodles to keep them from sticking.

Wash and prepare all of the vegetables, placing them in a large, oiled roasting pan. Pour the olive oil over them and sprinkle with sea salt and freshly ground pepper. Add the herbs and toss well to coat the vegetables thoroughly. Place the roasting pan in the oven and bake for 35–40 minutes, stirring occasionally. When the vegetables are fork-tender, remove from the oven and gently stir in the beans and artichoke hearts.

Oil the bottom of a lasagna-style baking dish. Spoon a little of the *Basic Fresh Marinara Sauce* (Autumn, page 119) into the bottom of the dish. Lay down 3 noodle strips, topping with a spoon of marinara sauce to moisten. Follow with a layer of vegetables, using about ½ of the mixture. Press down snugly. Cover with more sauce, then pieces of goat cheese. Repeat with noodles, vegetables, sauce, and cheese. Top with the last 3 noodles, sauce, and pieces of cheese. (I always sprinkle extra herbs on the top as well.)

Bake for about 35 minutes, or until the lasagna is hot and bubbling. It is best to let the lasagna sit for about 10 minutes before you cut and serve.

Enjoy with a bitter green salad tossed with ripe olives and *Balsamic Vinaigrette* (Winter, page 186) with a basket of warm Italian bread.

Serves 6.

Basic Fresh Marinara Sauce

Every Goddess needs to know how to whip up a basic red sauce.

2 tablespoons extra-virgin olive oil

1 onion, diced

2 tablespoons tomato paste (sun-dried paste is excellent)

6 garlic cloves, crushed

½ cup hot water

6 roma tomatoes, chopped

1 can (28 ounces) Italian plum tomatoes

¼ cup red wine

1 teaspoon sea salt

1–2 teaspoons sugar

1 bay leaf

2 teaspoons marjoram

2 tablespoons chopped fresh basil

2 tablespoons chopped fresh Italian parsley

In a large heavy pot, heat the olive oil over medium heat and sauté the onions for 5 minutes. Add the tomato paste and garlic and stir-fry with a wooden spoon for 3–4 minutes. Add the hot water and stir to thin the paste. Add the roma tomatoes, canned tomatoes, wine, sea salt, sugar, bay leaf, and herbs.

Turn up the heat and bring the sauce to a high simmer, then lower the heat to cook slowly, stirring occasionally. Taste for seasoning adjustments. Simmer your sauce on low heat for at least 1 hour. The longer it cooks, the more it reduces and intensifies the flavor.

Serving ideas

- This versatile, fresh tasting sauce can be used in any recipe calling for tomato sauce. It is also a wonderful, classic sauce for your favorite pasta.

- For a chunkier aromatic sauce, try adding:

  1 cup sliced cremini mushrooms
  1–2 teaspoons fresh rosemary, chopped
  ½ cup sliced black (ripe) olives

Follow the directions above, adding the mushrooms and rosemary into the onions, sautéing them before adding the tomato paste. Continue as directed, and add in the olives as the last ingredient.

Note your favorite additions to this sauce:

Tri-Colored Stuffed Peppers

Create some Equinox magick by stuffing yellow peppers for creativity, red peppers for vitality and strength, and green peppers for prosperity. The yummy stuffing is Spanish rice, laced with chile flavor and crunchy pine nuts.

2   tablespoons extra-virgin olive oil
1   Spanish onion, diced
5   garlic cloves, minced
1   cup chopped mushrooms
4   roma tomatoes, chopped
½   teaspoon curry powder
½   cup pine nuts
2½–3 cups prepared *Spanish Rice*
2   tablespoons fresh chopped cilantro or parsley
3   large bell peppers (1 green, 1 yellow, 1 red), halved, seeded
1   cup *Basic Fresh Marinara Sauce*
½   cup of your favorite salsa
6   slices of feta cheese or soy cheddar cheese

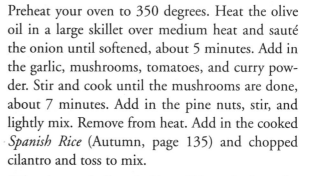

Preheat your oven to 350 degrees. Heat the olive oil in a large skillet over medium heat and sauté the onion until softened, about 5 minutes. Add in the garlic, mushrooms, tomatoes, and curry powder. Stir and cook until the mushrooms are done, about 7 minutes. Add in the pine nuts, stir, and lightly mix. Remove from heat. Add in the cooked *Spanish Rice* (Autumn, page 135) and chopped cilantro and toss to mix.

Oil a large, shallow baking dish and place the halved peppers, cut side up, in alternating colors. Stuff the peppers with the rice mixture, pressing in firmly.

Combine the *Basic Fresh Marinara Sauce* (Autumn, page 119) with ½ cup of salsa and mix well. Top each pepper with a generous spoonful of this spicy marinara sauce and a slice of feta cheese. Pour about an inch of water into the bottom of the baking pan and loosely cover with foil.

Bake for about 35–45 minutes, until the peppers are fork-tender.

Serves 6 (one stuffed pepper per person).

Bread Crumb Pasta for Two

A simple, satisfying pasta that can be easily thrown together on those nights when there is "nothing in the pantry." Magick happens!

½ pound Italian linguini

4 tablespoons extra-virgin olive oil

4 garlic cloves, minced

½ cup Italian-style seasoned bread crumbs

½ cup chopped fresh Italian parsley

¼ cup grated Parmesan cheese

2 tablespoons grated Romano cheese

Bring a large pot of salted water to a rolling boil and cook the pasta till al dente. In a large skillet, heat the olive oil over medium-low heat and toss in the garlic. Add in the bread crumbs and stir well, until the bread crumbs begin to brown.

Drain the cooked pasta and pour it into the skillet. Toss it with the toasted bread crumbs and garlic, coating the linguini well. Add in the chopped parsley and cheeses and lightly toss to coat evenly.

Serves 2.

Serving ideas

• Serve in a warm dish, paired with *Cauliflower Baked with Wine and Tomatoes* (Autumn, page 136) or topped with a generous spoonful of *Roasted Winter Vegetables* (Winter, page 181).

Roasted Acorn Squash Risotto

Whichever Italian Goddess first created risotto, a wonderfully creamy, flavorful rice dish, I am indebted to her. If you love acorn squash as much as I do, you will adore this risotto, infused with the flavor of nutmeg, accented with the spicy-sweet flavor of vegetarian "sausage."

1	acorn squash, halved, seeded
8	vegetarian sausage patties
2	tablespoons extra-virgin olive oil
½	sweet onion, diced
3	garlic cloves, minced
½	teaspoon curry powder
¼	teaspoon Chinese five-spice powder
¼	teaspoon nutmeg
1½	cups Italian arborio rice, uncooked
½	cup dry sherry
3	cups vegetable broth plus ½ cup water, heated
½	cup slivered pecans
2	tablespoons half-and-half or soy cream
	Black pepper, freshly ground
1	tablespoon chopped fresh parsley
	Pecans

Preheat your oven to 400 degrees. Roast the squash by placing the two halves, cut side down, on a well-oiled baking sheet. Bake for about 30 minutes, or until fork-tender. Remove from the oven and cool for a few minutes. Scoop out the roasted squash and set aside.

Spray a nonstick skillet with olive oil and, over medium heat, gently fry the sausages, until they are golden brown. Remove from heat and set aside.

In a heavy saucepan, heat the olive oil over medium heat and sauté the onion and garlic for 3 minutes. Add the curry, spices, and uncooked arborio rice and stir well, until the rice is coated. Stir and cook for about 5 minutes. Add the sherry and 1 cup of the broth and bring to a boil. Reduce heat and simmer uncovered, stirring frequently for 7–8 minutes.

When most of the liquid is absorbed, add the remaining cups of broth 1 cup at a time, stirring and simmering until each cup of liquid is absorbed before adding the next one. (The whole process should take about 20–25 minutes.) When the final cup of liquid is mostly absorbed, add the roasted squash and pecans and mix well. Break up the sausages into bite-size pieces and toss them in.

Continue stirring with a wooden spoon, until the rice is creamy, yet still retains some "bite." Add the half-and-half, if you desire extra creaminess, and stir well. Add freshly ground pepper and set aside for a few moments before serving. Spoon into four warmed bowls and garnish with chopped parsley and pecans.

Serves 4.

Country-Style Garlic Polenta

This is our son Alexander's current favorite version of polenta . . . when we can tear him away from one of his many creative projects.

4 cups vegetable broth, plus 2 cups fresh water

1½ cups stone-ground polenta cornmeal

⅛ teaspoon sea salt

6 garlic cloves, minced

1 teaspoon marjoram

1 teaspoon basil

Soy cream or milk (optional)

3 cups *Basic Fresh Marinara Sauce*, heated

½ cup shaved Reggiano Parmesan cheese

4 tablespoons chopped fresh parsley

In a heavy soup pot, bring the vegetable broth and water to a boil. Slowly pour the cornmeal into the broth in a steady stream, stirring constantly with a wire whisk. Reduce the heat to low and stir in the salt, garlic, and herbs, continuing to stir with a wooden spoon. Stir and cook the cornmeal mush for about 20–25 minutes. (You may add a dash of milk or soy cream here for even more creaminess, if you desire.) The polenta is done when it begins to pull away from the side of the pot.

Serve this creamy-style polenta by spooning it immediately into warmed bowls. Top with a generous spoonful of heated *Basic Fresh Marinara Sauce* (Autumn, page 119) and garnish with shaved Reggiano Parmesan and freshly chopped parsley.

Serves 4.

Baked Shells with Broccoli and Tomato

Shorter days and chilly evenings make even Vegan Goddesses crave comfort food. So here is my satisfying vegan version of Mom's macaroni and cheese, without the dairy.

1	pound Italian medium-sized shell pasta
2	tablespoons extra-virgin olive oil
2	tablespoons unbleached flour
1½	cups plain almond or nondairy milk
½	teaspoon Dijon mustard
2	tablespoons dry sherry
	Black pepper, freshly ground
	Nutmeg
1	cup grated soy cheese, cheddar or jack style
1	tablespoon extra-virgin olive oil
1½	cups broccoli florets
2	tablespoons extra-virgin olive oil
3	garlic cloves, minced
¼	cup Italian seasoned bread crumbs
4	roma tomatoes, sliced
1–2	tablespoons chopped fresh parsley

Bring a large pot of fresh water to a rolling boil and cook the pasta shells until barely al dente. You do not want to overcook the pasta, as it will continue cooking in the casserole. Drain and rinse in cool water when it is done. Set aside.

To make the cheese sauce, heat the olive oil over low-medium heat in a heavy sauce pan. Stir in the flour with a wooden spoon, stirring and cooking the flour for 5 minutes. When the paste thickens and bubbles, slowly begin to add the milk, stirring constantly to blend. (I like to use a whisk for this.) Keep stirring and heating the sauce. Add in the mustard, sherry, pepper, and a pinch of nutmeg.

When the sauce is thickened and heated through, add the grated soy cheese and stir well, until the cheese is melted. Reduce the heat to low.

Preheat oven to 350 degrees. To make your casserole, pour the cooked pasta into an oiled casserole dish. In a medium skillet, heat 1 tablespoon olive oil over medium heat and lightly sauté the broccoli florets for 3–4 minutes, until tender-crisp.

Remove from heat and add the broccoli to the cheese sauce. Mix gently and pour the sauce into the casserole dish, stirring the pasta shells thoroughly to mix in the sauce and broccoli pieces. In the same skillet, heat 2 tablespoons of olive oil and sauté the garlic and bread crumbs, until the

continued

crumbs are well coated. Arrange the sliced tomatoes across the top of the casserole. Spoon the crumb-garlic mixture on top of the tomato slices.

Bake the casserole for 20–30 minutes, until the sauce is hot and bubbly and the bread crumb topping is browned. Remove from the oven and sprinkle with chopped parsley. Let the casserole sit for 5 minutes before serving.

Serve with a mixed green salad dressed in *Dijon Vinaigrette* (Winter, page 185) and some warm cornbread. There now, don't you feel better?

Serves 4–6.

Serving idea

• This creamy sauce is also wonderful on cooked fettuccine.

Stuffed Acorn Squash

This fragrant autumn dish makes a wonderful alternative to stuffed poultry over the holidays. It is visually beautiful and combines well with other traditional holiday foods.

2   tablespoons extra-virgin olive oil

1   medium onion, diced

1   celery stalk, chopped

1   cup sliced mushrooms

¼   cup pine nuts

¼   cup dried cranberries

1   tablespoon chopped fresh parsley

1   teaspoon curry powder

   Sea salt

   Black pepper, freshly ground

2   tablespoons dry sherry

2   cups cornbread stuffing

¾   cup boiling water

3   medium-large acorn squash, halved, seeded

Preheat oven to 350 degrees. In a large skillet, heat the olive oil over medium heat. Add the onion and celery and sauté for 5 minutes. Add in the mushrooms and pine nuts and stir, cooking until the vegetables are soft, about 7 minutes. Add in the cranberries, parsley, curry, sea salt, pepper, and dry sherry. Mix well and remove from heat.

Mix in the dry stuffing with the vegetables and seasonings. Slowly add in the hot water, a little at a time, stirring the stuffing to moisten. When the stuffing is moist but not soggy, set aside.

Place the halved squash, cut side up, in a large, oiled roasting pan. Stuff the squash generously and press the stuffing in firmly. Pour an inch or two of hot water into the bottom of the pan to keep the squash from sticking to the pan. (If there is stuffing left over, place it in a small, oiled baking dish and bake it along with the stuffed squash.) Bake for 45–55 minutes, until the squash is fork-tender and the stuffing is cooked through.

Serve with a soup and *Mesclun Salad with Apples and Toasted Walnuts* in a *Ginger Citrus Vinaigrette* (Autumn, page 139).

Serves 6.

Skillet Supper (Beans and Rice with Vegetables in Red Wine)

This is a heart-warming, one-pot supper that I have been cooking and adjusting for many years. It goes together rather quickly, which any busy Goddess will appreciate. Feel free to substitute any of the vegetables for ones you may already have on hand.

2 tablespoons extra-virgin olive oil

1 yellow onion, diced

6 garlic cloves, minced

6–7 roma tomatoes, chopped

1 portobello mushroom, stemmed, sliced

1 yellow pepper, cored, seeded, chopped

1 cup small broccoli florets

1 cup uncooked brown rice

3 cups vegetable broth

½ cup red wine

Sea salt

Black pepper, freshly ground

½ teaspoon marjoram

½ teaspoon Italian herbs

2 tablespoons chopped fresh parsley

1 cup canned black beans, drained, rinsed,

4–5 ounces feta cheese, crumbled

In a large skillet, heat the olive oil over medium heat and sauté the onion, for about 5 minutes. Add in the garlic, tomatoes, mushrooms, pepper, broccoli, and uncooked rice. Stir and sauté for about 10 minutes, coating the rice with the seasoned olive oil and mixing in the vegetables. Pour in the broth and red wine, adding the sea salt and pepper to taste. Add the herbs.

Cover tightly and bring to a boil. Lower the heat and simmer gently for 45 minutes. Stir in the black beans and sprinkle with the crumbled feta cheese. Cover and heat through on low for 5 minutes.

Serve this satisfying one-dish supper with a basket of grilled cornbread.

Serves 4.

Corn Pancakes with Black Bean Salsa

Perfect for an autumn brunch or casual supper, these delicious savory pancakes are a real Goddess favorite. The Black Bean Salsa makes a spicy accompaniment.

1½ cups stone-ground cornmeal

⅔ cup unbleached flour

2 teaspoons baking powder

1 teaspoon sea salt

1 tablespoon sugar

¼ teaspoon chili powder

2 cups plain soy milk or milk

4 tablespoons canola oil

2 free-range eggs or egg substitute

1 cup Mexican-style corn, drained

4 scallions, sliced

½–1 teaspoon red pepper flakes

2 tablespoons finely chopped cilantro

Black Bean Salsa

Creamy Savory Sauce

Preheat your griddle to 375 degrees. In a large mixing bowl, combine the dry ingredients and stir together well. In another bowl, combine the soy milk, oil, and eggs. Mix well. Pour the wet ingredients into the dry ingredients and stir together, until well moistened. The pancake batter will be thin. Stir in the corn, scallions, red pepper flakes, and cilantro.

Using a ¼-cup measuring cup, measure and pour ¼ cup of the pancake batter onto your hot griddle. Repeat for as many pancakes as you can fit on your griddle. Cook each pancake until some of the air bubbles in the batter pop.

Flip the pancakes and cook another 2–3 minutes, until the underside is nicely browned. If not serving immediately, keep the pancakes warm on an ovenproof plate in a 200-degree oven, until you are ready to serve.

continued

Serve the corn pancakes with small bowls of *Black Bean Salsa* and *Creamy Savory Sauce* on the side. *Serves 4.*

Black Bean Salsa

A spicy side dish, perfect for the Corn Pancakes or any Southwestern main dish.

Combine all of the ingredients in a bowl, cover, and chill for 1 hour. Serve at room temperature. May be made up ahead of time and chilled overnight.

Creamy Savory Sauce

Combine the sour cream, lime juice, garlic, and good-sized pinches of all the spices and stir. Add a little soy milk to thin, if necessary. Heat gently in a small saucepan till warmed through. Serve with the corn pancakes as a sauce.

Black Bean Salsa

- 1 can (1 pound) black beans, drained, rinsed
- 4 garlic cloves, minced
- ½ small red onion, finely chopped
- 1 cup chopped tomatoes (may be canned)
- 1 small jalapeño pepper, seeded, chopped fine
- 1 teaspoon extra-virgin olive oil
- 1 teaspoon balsamic vinegar
- 1 teaspoon cumin
- 1–2 tablespoons fresh chopped cilantro

Creamy Savory Sauce

- ¾ cup light sour cream or plain yogurt
- Juice of ½ lime
- 1 garlic clove, minced
- Cayenne pepper
- Cumin
- Cinnamon
- Plain soy milk (for thinning)

Middle Eastern Plate

No Goddess can resist the flavors of this Middle Eastern-inspired dish. Splendid colorful vegetables form a mosaic of flavor against pearly white couscous and creamy hummus. Roasting brings out the natural sweetness in peppers, onions, and squash that beautifully counterpoints the exotic spices in this wonderful dish.

2 cups cut green beans, blanched for 1 minute, then plunged into ice water, drained

1 large onion, cut in chunks

1 eggplant, peeled, sliced, cut into triangles

6 roma tomatoes, cut in half lengthwise

1 yellow pepper, cored, seeded, cut into strips

½ butternut squash, peeled, cubed

10 garlic cloves, peeled

3 tablespoons extra-virgin olive oil

1 teaspoon fennel
Sea salt
White pepper, freshly ground

1–2 tablespoons fresh chopped mint
Couscous
Spicy Hummus

4 fresh pita breads, cut into triangles

Preheat your oven to 375 degrees. In a large roasting pan, combine all of the vegetables, garlic, and olive oil. Add the fennel, salt, and pepper. Roast for 35–45 minutes or until veggies are tender. Sprinkle them with fresh mint and set aside.

To serve, spoon the *Couscous* (page 131) onto individual plates, and top with the roasted vegetables. Spoon a scoop of *Spicy Hummus* (Autumn, page 105) on the side, and edge the plate with triangles of fresh pita bread.

Serves 4.

continued

Couscous

Bring the water to a boil in a nonstick saucepan, and add a pinch of sea salt and the olive oil. Stir in couscous. Cover and remove pan from heat. Allow the couscous to sit for 10 minutes, until all the liquid is absorbed. Fluff with a fork to separate the grains before serving.

Couscous
1¼ cups water
Sea salt
1 teaspoon extra-virgin olive oil
1 cup uncooked couscous

Roasted Vegetable Pizza

Roasting the vegetables first gives added dimension to this favorite classic. We make pizzas in our family every Friday evening. It's become an absolute tradition. (Goddesses love making traditions.)

1	sweet onion, sliced into chunks
½	large red pepper, cored, seeded, cut into strips
½	yellow pepper, cored, seeded, cut into strips
1	cup broccoli florets
6	garlic cloves, peeled, sliced
3	tablespoons extra-virgin olive oil
1	teaspoon marjoram
1	teaspoon rosemary
	Sea salt
	Black pepper, freshly ground
	Prepared *Pizza Dough*
	Cornmeal
¼	cup *Basic Fresh Marinara Sauce*
¼	cup pine nuts
4–6	ounces feta cheese, cut into cubes

Preheat your oven to 400 degrees. In an oiled roasting pan, combine the vegetables and toss them in the olive oil to coat evenly. Sprinkle with the herbs and seasonings. Roast in the oven for about 15 minutes, until vegetables are just tender-crisp. Remove from the oven and set aside.

Take the prepared *Pizza Dough* (Spring, page 26) and spread it on a pizza pan dusted with cornmeal. (If you are using a pizza stone, preheat the stone while you prepare the pizza dough on a floured peel.)

Spoon on the *Basic Fresh Marinara Sauce* (Autumn, page 119). Add the roasted vegetables, sprinkle with the pine nuts, and dot with cubed feta cheese. Drizzle a little extra-virgin olive oil around the edges of the crust. (If using a pizza stone, lightly dust the preheated stone with cornmeal, and slide your pizza onto the stone.)

Place your pizza in the oven. Bake at 400 degrees for about 20 minutes, until the crust is golden brown and at the desired crispness.

Serves 2–4, depending on appetite!

Roasted Vegetable Burritos

Some Goddesses like their vegetables steamed, but when it comes to stuffing a burrito, I prefer roasted vegetables and their greater depth of flavor.

1	large red onion, cut into chunks
1	yam or sweet potato, peeled, cubed
3	red potatoes, scrubbed, cubed
1	cup broccoli florets, cut into bite-size pieces
3	carrots, peeled, julienned
1	cup sweet corn (frozen is fine)
2–3	tablespoons extra-virgin olive oil
8	garlic cloves, sliced
½	teaspoon cumin
½	teaspoon curry powder
½	teaspoon chili powder
6	large burrito-size flour tortillas
	Light sour cream or soy yogurt (optional)
	Salsa (optional)

Preheat your oven to 400 degrees. In a large, oiled roasting pan, combine all the vegetables with the olive oil, garlic, and spices, stirring to coat evenly. Bake for 20–30 minutes, or until the vegetables are fork-tender and slightly browned. Check and stir them occasionally to keep them from sticking to the pan.

Wrap the tortillas in foil and heat them in the oven during the last 5 minutes of the vegetables' roasting time, just to warm them.

Lay your first tortilla on a warm plate and spoon ⅙ of the vegetables lengthwise in the center. Add a spoonful of sour cream and salsa, if desired. Wrap up by folding in the ends just over the edge of the filling, then wrap rolling lengthwise to make your burrito.

Serves 6.

Serving ideas

- Serve with extra salsa, *Spanish Rice* (Autumn, page 135), and warmed pinto beans on the side, or enjoy these burritos with a bowl of yummy *Winter Solstice Pumpkin Soup* (Winter, page 160).

Coconut-Curried Vegetable Stew

If you love the warm and spicy flavor of curry, try this beautiful vegetable stew. Impressive and complex in flavors and texture, it actually is quite simple to put together. Perfect for any Goddess gathering!

2	tablespoons canola oil
1	medium yellow onion, chopped
4	garlic cloves, chopped
2	tablespoons curry powder
½	teaspoon Chinese five-spice powder
4	carrots, scrubbed, sliced into chunks
½	head cauliflower, cored, cut into bite-size pieces
1½	cups cubed butternut squash
2	medium new potatoes, peeled, thinly sliced
2	cups vegetable broth
1	teaspoon sugar
1	can (14 ounces) light coconut milk
1	cup green peas, (frozen)
1	can (16 ounces) chickpeas, drained, rinsed
	Black pepper, freshly ground
2½–3	cups cooked basmati rice

In a heavy soup pot, heat the oil over medium heat and sauté the onion until soft. Lower the heat and stir in the garlic and spices, cooking for 1–2 minutes. Add in the carrots, cauliflower, squash, and potatoes. Stir well to coat with the spices and cook for 3 minutes. Add in the broth and sugar and bring to a gentle simmer. Lower the heat and cover, gently simmering for about 15 minutes.

Stir in the coconut milk and peas. Simmer until the vegetables are tender, for about 10 more minutes or so. Add in the chickpeas and stir. Taste for seasoning adjustments, adding the freshly ground pepper. Heat through for 5 minutes and serve immediately.

Serve this deliciously spicy-sweet curry over a scoop of hot basmati rice in a warmed soup plate.

Serves 6.

Savory Sides

Spanish Rice

A warming, festive side dish that accents the humble pinto bean beautifully . . . a favorite combo of the Corn Mother Goddess. Serve it with burritos, enchiladas, and tacos, of course, but it also pairs equally well with dishes such as Tofu Scramble.

2	cups tomato juice
½	cup water
1	cup Texmati rice, uncooked
2	teaspoons olive oil
1	teaspoon chili powder
½	teaspoon cumin
3	green onions, chopped

Steamer: If you are using a rice steamer, which I absolutely swear by, simply combine all of the ingredients in the bowl and follow your manufacturer's instructions.

Stove top: Bring the tomato juice and water to a boil in a nonstick saucepan. Stir in the rice, olive oil, spices, and onions. Cover and reduce heat to low, simmering until all of the liquid is absorbed, about 25–30 minutes. Stir and fluff with a fork before serving.

Serves 4.

Serving idea

- To serve with *Tofu Scramble*, see Spring, page 31.

Cauliflower Baked with Wine and Tomatoes

Even those who are not particularly fond of cauliflower may be tempted by this tasty baked casserole infused with the flavors of garlic, wine, rosemary, and capers. Serve it on the night of the Wine Moon and toast Hathor, the Egyptian Sky Goddess of love, art, and beauty.

2   tablespoons extra-virgin olive oil

1   large onion, sliced

6   garlic cloves, minced

4   cups chopped cauliflower

1   can (28 ounces) Italian plum tomatoes, coarsely chopped, with liquid

½   cup dry red wine

2   tablespoons capers, rinsed

1   teaspoon rosemary

2   tablespoons chopped fresh Italian parsley

Sea salt

Black pepper, freshly ground

Asiago cheese, freshly shredded

Preheat your oven to 350 degrees. Heat the olive oil in a large skillet over medium heat and sauté the onion for 5 minutes, until soft. Add the garlic and cauliflower and sauté for 3–5 minutes. Remove from heat. Add the tomatoes, wine, capers, herbs, sea salt, and pepper. Mix well.

Pour the vegetable mixture into an oiled baking dish. Top with shredded Asiago. Bake for 30–35 minutes, or until the cauliflower is fork-tender and the sauce is bubbling.

Serves 4–6.

Serving idea

- Serve with the *Bread Crumb Pasta for Two* (Autumn, page 121) or steamed basmati rice.

Whipped Sweet Potatoes with Coconut Milk

My sister Lori, a kitty-loving Goddess who loves to garden and write, created this recipe to dispel her own myth that she disliked sweet potatoes. Once you try these exotically creamy sweet potatoes, you'll throw away those mini-marshmallows forever.

4   medium sweet potatoes, skinned, cubed
    Sea salt
    Black pepper, freshly ground
2   pats of butter or soy margarine
2   teaspoons freshly grated ginger
    Light coconut milk

Place the sweet potatoes in a pot and cover with fresh water. Bring to a boil and simmer the potatoes, until they are fork-tender, about 20 minutes. Drain the potatoes well and return to the pot. Season with sea salt and pepper and butter. Add in the grated ginger. Mix with a fork to soften the potatoes.

Add the coconut milk slowly, stirring it in with a whisk, just until the sweet potatoes are smooth and creamy. Taste for seasoning adjustments.

Serves 4.

Autumn Salads

Mesclun Salad with Apples and Toasted Walnuts

Here is a beautiful salad, with tart apples and crunchy toasted walnuts, to complement any Autumn feast. The Ginger Citrus Vinaigrette adds savory citrus flavor that also helps to keep the apples fresh.

6 cups mesclun salad mix
½ red onion, sliced thin
1 tart apple, peeled, cored, diced
2 tablespoons raisins
¼ cup walnut pieces, lightly toasted on a baking sheet

Ginger Citrus Vinaigrette
2 tablespoons sesame oil
1 tablespoon lime juice
1 tablespoon lemon juice
Curry powder
½ teaspoon fresh minced ginger
Sea salt
Black pepper, freshly ground

Combine salad ingredients in a chilled salad bowl and dress with the *Ginger Citrus Vinaigrette* (below). *Serves 4.*

Ginger Citrus Vinaigrette

A slightly spicy, gingery vinaigrette, perfect for giving greens an exotic twist of flavor.

Blend ingredients well and pour on salad greens.

Salad Greens and Oranges with Raspberry Vinaigrette

Mix of salad greens
1 chilled orange, peeled, sectioned, pith removed
½ red onion, peeled, diced fine
½ cup chopped black olives

Raspberry Vinaigrette
2 tablespoons light sesame oil
2 tablespoons raspberry vinegar
1 teaspoon sugar
½ teaspoon lemon zest

Fill a bowl with fresh salad greens and toss in the orange slices, chopped onions, and olives. Make the *Raspberry Vinaigrette* dressing (below) and drizzle over the salad and serve.

Raspberry Vinaigrette

Combine all of the dressing ingredients and whisk together. Drizzle over the salad and serve.

Sweet Endings

Buttermilk Cake

A sweet indulgence during those shorter days of fall to share over coffee after a brisk walk through falling leaves.

2 cups unbleached all-purpose flour
1 cup sugar
½ cup brown sugar
1 teaspoon baking soda
1 teaspoon baking powder
½ teaspoon salt
1 teaspoon cinnamon
1 cup buttermilk
2 free-range eggs
⅔ cup canola oil
1 teaspoon bourbon vanilla
½ cup brown sugar
½ cup chopped walnuts
1 teaspoon cinnamon
½ teaspoon nutmeg

Preheat oven to 350 degrees. In a large mixing bowl, combine the flour, sugars, baking soda, baking powder, salt, and cinnamon. In a separate bowl, combine the buttermilk, eggs, canola oil, and vanilla, blending well. Add the wet ingredients into the flour mixture, and stir just until moistened. Don't overbeat the batter. Pour the batter into a greased 9 by 13-inch glass baking pan.

Make your topping, combining the brown sugar, chopped nuts, and spices. Mix well. Crumble the topping evenly over the cake batter.

Bake for about 30 minutes, or until a toothpick inserted into the center emerges clean. Let the cake cool on a wire rack.

Serve right out of the pan, placing a square of the cake onto a dessert plate, accompanied by a soft scoop of *Maple Ice Cream* (Autumn, page 142).

Serves 8.

Maple Ice Cream

This cold and creamy maple confection is the perfect compliment to a slice of simple cake still warm from the oven. Or you can top it with walnuts for a classic maple-walnut treat.

½ cup whipping cream or nondairy cream

1½ cups milk or almond milk

4 ounces pasteurized egg substitute

¾ cup real maple syrup Bourbon vanilla extract

¼ teaspoon xanthan gum

Combine the cream, milk, egg substitute, maple syrup, and a dash of vanilla in a blender. Whip until smooth and frothy. Add in the xanthan gum and blend. Pour into an ice cream maker and freeze according to manufacturer's guidelines.

To store, scoop ice cream into a plastic container with a strong lid and keep in the freezer. Slightly soften the ice cream before serving.

Note: I use a pasteurized egg substitute such as Egg Beaters in my frozen dessert recipes, not only because they are fat and cholesterol-free, but safer as well. Raw eggs may contain harmful bacteria. I do not ever recommend using unpastuerized raw eggs in an ice cream recipe.

Serves 4.

Apple Cranberry Crisp

The sweet cinnamon aroma that fills the house while this timeless dessert bakes in the oven is a perfect way to welcome in the Celtic New Year. Apples are the fruit of the Goddess and one of the true pleasures of Autumn. Crisp, tart Granny Smiths are my favorite apples to use in baking.

2	pounds tart, crisp apples (such as Granny Smith)
¼	cup apple juice
	Squeeze of lemon juice
½	cup fresh cranberries or dried, sweetened
½	cup brown sugar
1	teaspoon cinnamon
½	teaspoon allspice
	Nutmeg
	Sea salt
½	cup unbleached flour
½	cup rolled oats
½	cup crushed ginger snaps
¼	cup brown sugar
1	teaspoon cinnamon
½	stick unsalted butter or margarine

Preheat your oven to 350 degrees. Peel, core, and slice the apples. In a large mixing bowl, combine the apples with the apple juice, lemon juice, cranberries, brown sugar, cinnamon, allspice, and a pinch of nutmeg and sea salt. Pour into a greased 2-quart baking dish.

To make the topping, mix together the flour, oats, ginger snaps, brown sugar, and cinnamon. Cut in dabs of the chilled butter, making a moist, crumbly mixture. Spoon the topping over the apples.

Cover the dish with a piece of foil and bake for 30 minutes. Uncover and continue baking for 30 minutes, until the apples are tender and the topping is crisp and golden brown.

Serve warm with a freshly brewed pot of clove and orange tea.

Serves 4–6.

Dense Lemon Cake in Chocolate-Cognac Sauce

What better way to end an evening meal—the palate-cleansing clarity of citrus with a kiss of dark chocolate sauce! This is a perfect Goddess dessert after enjoying a hearty autumn meal laced with onion and garlic.

1 cup unsalted butter or stick margarine

1 cup sugar

4 free-range eggs, lightly beaten

1½ tablespoons lemon zest

1 teaspoon bourbon vanilla

1 cup sour cream

2½ cups unbleached all-purpose flour

1 teaspoon baking powder

1 teaspoon baking soda

¼ teaspoon salt

½ cup finely chopped walnuts

½ cup fresh lemon juice

½ cup sugar

Preheat oven to 350 degrees. In a large mixing bowl, cream the butter and sugar. Add in the eggs and beat until creamy. Add in the lemon zest, vanilla, and sour cream. In a separate bowl, mix together the flour, baking powder, baking soda, and salt. Slowly add these dry ingredients into the wet egg mixture. Gently stir in the walnuts.

Pour the cake batter into a large, greased loaf pan and bake for about 55 minutes, or until a toothpick inserted into the center emerges clean. Remove the cake from the oven and allow it to rest for 5 minutes.

In a small nonreactive saucepan, combine the lemon juice and sugar and bring to a boil. Reduce heat and simmer the sauce for 5 more minutes, until it becomes a syrup. Spoon the lemon syrup generously over the entire top surface of the cake. Set aside to cool.

When cooled, remove the cake from the pan and place on a cake plate. Serve slices on dessert plates decoratively drizzled with the *Chocolate-Cognac Sauce* (page 145).

Serves 10.

continued

Chocolate-Cognac Sauce

A quick and easy chocolate sauce that Goddesses love to drizzle on everything from lemon cake to home-made ice cream.

If you have a microwave, heat up the milk in a Pyrex cup till bubbling. On the stovetop, using a double boiler or a heavy saucepan, gently heat the milk on low till bubbling, taking care not to scorch. Remove from heat and stir in the chocolate. When it is completely melted, add in the Grand Marnier and stir well. Serve immediately. Keep leftover sauce in an airtight container, refrigerated, up to 1 week.

Note: For a non-alcoholic sauce, simply substitute cold coffee or milk instead.

Chocolate-Cognac Sauce
- ½ cup sweetened condensed milk
- 4 ounces Ghirardelli semisweet chocolate (chips or bar)
- 3 tablespoons Grand Marnier, Cointreau, or Cognac

Bread Pudding

After your Autumn feast, serve this creamy, old-fashioned dessert and step outside to watch the stars glittering in the dark blue sky. Make a wish.

4 cups milk or vanilla-almond milk

4 free-range eggs

2 teaspoons Mexican vanilla extract

½ cup honey

4 cups cubed stale egg or oatmeal bread, crusts removed

½ cup currants or raisins

½ teaspoon nutmeg

1 teaspoon cinnamon

½ cup almond slivers, toasted

Preheat your oven to 350 degrees. Lightly oil a 2-quart baking dish. Combine the milk, eggs, vanilla, and honey in a large mixing bowl. Beat together well. Add in the bread cubes and let them soak for 10 minutes. Add in the currants and spices, mix well, and pour into the prepared baking dish.

Bake for 1 hour, or until the pudding is set and lightly browned on top. Remove from the oven and sprinkle with the toasted almonds. Serve slightly warm.

Serves 4–6.

Notes on your favorite
Autumn recipes

In approaching the four seasons as aspects of the Goddess, we end (and begin) our circle with midwinter, the **solstice**, when she emerges as the virgin, complete unto herself, the original meaning of the word virgin. We celebrate the birth of the **divine** child, and hope returns with the lengthening rays of the sun. By February the virgin becomes the bride, in her **shimmering** white, anticipating the arrival of her beloved, the Sun God, and we join her in eagerness for signs of spring.

Our Wheel of the Year's four seasons also contain the **circle** of the four directions and the corresponding four elements. In winter the Goddess stands in the north, dressed in **white**. Her element is earth. We meditate upon her stillness, her stark white **beauty**, and ground ourselves with introspection, study, and nourishment. We gravitate towards **warming**, grounding, earthy foods and spices. It is a time to look inward, find stillness, and surrender to the Goddess' wisdom.

Winter

Festival Menus

Winter Solstice (aka Yule)

On the longest night of the year we gather to rejoice . . . for at this moment the sun will begin his return to us, inch by inch. The Goddess has spent her dark nights as Hecate, the Crone, and emerges as Mary, the Star of the Sea, to give birth to the Sun Child.

Light your home and hearth with burning candles of red and gold to honor the warming rays of the sun. Decorate with evergreens that remind us the Goddess indeed lives. Even through the winter dark, her green life is present. Holly, balsam, cedar, and ivy are her gifts of the season. This is a time for feasting and joy, for the longest dark has passed, and hope again returns.

Mulled Wine *(page 153)*

Baked Goat Cheese with Salsa on Crostini *(page 154)*

Winter Solstice Pumpkin Soup *(page 160)*

Red, White, and Green Lasagna *(page 171)*

Hazelnut Ice Cream *(page 190)*

Candlemas (aka Imbolc)

On the eve of February second we celebrate the promise of Candlemas, or Imbolc, the moment of the year when the days are getting noticeably longer and the new lambs are born. Snow drops push through the crust of snow and we eagerly await the return of the sun's warmth in spring. The Celtic Goddess Brigid comes to us as the Bride, awaiting the return of her lover, the sun. Adorned in her winter white she sparkles in her innocence and expectation.

It is time to begin seeds indoors, and clear out closets. Light a yellow candle in the center of a shallow bowl filled with snow to symbolize the warmth of the sun melting away the winter chill. Feed our feathered friends, the winged ones, with seed and grain.

White Bean Hummus with Capers and Dill *(page 155)*
Potato and Carrot Soup *(page 158)*
Irish Soda Bread *(page 156)*
Linguini with White Vegetables and Pine Nuts *(page 168)*
Chilled Winter Greens in Balsamic Vinaigrette *(page 186)*
Pear Crisp *(page 191)*

Beverages and Bites

Mulled Wine

A Yule tradition to warm up the festivities and brighten spirits!

1   bottle red wine,
      Burgundy or
      cabernet
1   cup orange juice,
      freshly squeezed
1   cup apple brandy
½   cup sugar
1   red apple, washed
      Cloves
1   orange, washed, sliced
      into rounds
4   cinnamon sticks

Gently combine wine, orange juice, brandy, and sugar in a large sauce pan and heat over low-medium heat. Stud the washed apple with cloves and float it in the mulled wine mixture, along with orange slices and cinnamon sticks. Keep at a low simmer for 15 minutes. Serve from a warm slow cooker or crock, if you have one, or heatproof serving bowl. Let the merrymaking begin!

Baked Goat Cheese with Salsa on Crostini

Melting snowy white goat cheese topped with festive red salsa . . . a warming start for the Yule celebration.

⅔ cup *Garlic Salsa* or favorite prepared salsa

4 garlic cloves, minced

3 roma tomatoes, chopped

2 tablespoons fresh cilantro or parsley, chopped

6–8 ounces chèvre or soft goat cheese

Crostini

1 French baguette

Preheat your oven to 350 degrees. In a small mixing bowl combine the *Garlic Salsa* (Summer, page 54) with the garlic, tomatoes, and cilantro. Mix well. In a small baking dish, spread the goat cheese first, then top with the salsa mixture.

Bake until heated through and bubbling, about 20 minutes. Make your *Crostini* (below).

Arrange the crostini around the hot goat cheese dish. Provide small spreading knives and napkins, and light the Yule Log!

Serves 4–6.

Crostini

Preheat your oven to 450 degrees. Slice across the baguette at a slight diagonal, cutting it into 1 to 1½-inch slices. Place the slices of the baguette on a cookie sheet, and toast them on each side in the oven, until lightly browned.

White Bean Hummus with Capers and Dill

Serve this delightful hummus as a dip for crisp celery crudités or toasted pita chips.

1 can (1 pound) white northern beans, drained, rinsed
4 garlic cloves, minced
¼ cup sesame tahini
Juice of 1 lemon
1 teaspoon cumin
1 teaspoon dill
Sea salt
White pepper, freshly ground
1 tablespoon capers, rinsed

Place about ¾ of the white beans into a blender and add minced garlic, tahini, lemon juice, cumin, dill, sea salt, and pepper. Cover and purée until smooth. Combine the purée with the remaining whole white beans and capers and mix well. Cover and chill for 1 hour or more.

Serve this creamy dip/spread slightly cool or at room temperature, garnished with a sprig of fresh dill and a few capers. Perfect with crudités or *Toasted Pita Chips* (Autumn, page 105).

Serves 6.

Irish Soda Bread

In bread we share kinship and celebrate sustenance. This flavorful Celtic classic has caraway for protection and love. The deep dark currants add sweetness to remind us that spring is on the way, and the cross design symbolizes the four directions.

2	cups unbleached all-purpose flour
4	tablespoons sugar
1	teaspoon baking powder
½	teaspoon baking soda
½	teaspoon sea salt
1	cup currants
1	tablespoon caraway seeds
1	free-range egg
¼	cup canola oil or melted stick margarine
⅔	cup milk or almond milk

Preheat oven to 375 degrees. Lightly grease a round cake pan with stick margarine. In a large bowl, combine the flour, sugar, baking powder and soda, salt, currants, and caraway seeds. Whisk together. In a separate bowl, whisk together the egg, oil, and milk. Pour into the dry ingredients and combine with a wooden spoon, until moistened. Batter will be a bit sticky.

Mound the batter onto the pan, forming a rounded-shape loaf in the center of the pan. Smooth out the surface as best you can. With a sharp knife, cut an equal-sized cross into the center-top surface, about ½-inch deep, and sprinkle lightly with flour.

Bake on the center rack for 25–30 minutes, until the loaf is a golden brown and a toothpick inserted into the center comes out clean. Place on a wire rack and cool before serving.

Cut the bread into wedges and serve in a basket, with plenty of butter or margarine.

Seasonal Soups

Spicy Black Bean Soup

An easy, hearty supper soup that goes together quickly, thanks to the canned black beans. Laced with the Caribbean flavors of lime and cayenne pepper, this delicious soup is guaranteed to "stick to your ribs," as Mother Goddesses like to say.

2 tablespoons extra-virgin olive oil
1 large red onion, diced
5 garlic cloves, minced
1 can (14 ounces) Mexican-style cut tomatoes
2 cups vegetable broth
½–1 cup water
4 cans (1 pound each) black beans, drained, rinsed
Juice of 2 limes
¼ cup dry sherry
1 teaspoon cumin
⅛–¼ teaspoon cayenne pepper
1 teaspoon dried cilantro
2 tablespoons chopped fresh parsley
Sea salt
Black pepper, freshly ground
2 cups cooked Texmati rice
Chopped chives or scallions
Lime wedges

In a heavy soup pot, heat the olive oil over medium heat and sauté the onion for 5 minutes. Add in the garlic and stir, cooking for 3 minutes. Add the tomatoes, broth, ½ cup water, black beans, lime juice, sherry, spices, and herbs. Mix well.

Turn up the heat and bring to a high simmer. Cover and lower the temperature to medium heat, simmering for 10 minutes. Check to see if you need to add more water to thin. Continue to slow simmer on low heat for 10–15 minutes.

To serve, ladle soup into soup plates and spoon a scoop of Texmati rice into the center of the bowl. Garnish with chives or chopped scallions and a wedge of lime. Hot crusty sourdough rolls complete the meal.

Serves 4.

Potato and Carrot Soup

A lovely potato soup to celebrate Brigid's emergence. Laced with sweet carrots and onion, this Celtic country soup warms the heart with the first promise of spring.

2 tablespoons extra-virgin olive oil
1 sweet onion, diced
4 carrots, peeled, sliced
½ head white cabbage, cored, thinly shredded
Nutmeg
¼ teaspoon curry powder
½ teaspoon fennel
Sea salt
White pepper, freshly ground
5 cups vegetable broth
6 Yukon Gold (or yellow) potatoes, peeled, cut
½ cup milk or nondairy cream
1–2 tablespoons light cream or soy cream
Fresh chives, chopped

In a heavy soup pot, heat the olive oil over medium heat and sauté the onion, until soft. Add the carrots, cabbage, spices, sea salt, and white pepper. Stir and cook for 10 minutes. Add in the vegetable broth and potatoes and bring to a boil over high heat. Lower heat and simmer until vegetables are tender, about 20–30 minutes.

When the vegetables are done, carefully ladle the soup mixture into a blender, reserving about a cup of the whole vegetable pieces in the soup pot. Cover the blender and purée the soup mixture until it is smooth, then pour the puréed soup back into the soup pot, stirring it together with the reserved vegetable pieces. Stir in ½ cup milk and gently heat it through, being careful not to bring the soup to a boil. Add the cream, if desired.

Ladle this creamy soup into colorful bowls and garnish with fresh chopped chives. Serve with *Irish Soda Bread* (Winter, page 156).

Serves 4–6.

Not-So-French Onion and Cabbage Soup

A sweet onion experience that you will easily take pleasure in, perhaps on some chilly day, gazing out of your window at softly falling snow, sipping some sherry while the cat curls up in your favorite chair.

2 tablespoons extra-virgin olive oil

5 medium onions, sliced into thin rings

½ head white cabbage, cored, thinly shredded

⅛ teaspoon rosemary

⅛ teaspoon thyme

1 teaspoon sugar
  Sea salt
  White pepper, freshly ground

1 tablespoon balsamic vinegar

5 cups vegetable broth

1 bay leaf

4 slices French bread
  Gruyère or soy cheese, shredded

In a heavy soup pot, heat the olive oil over medium heat and sauté the sliced onions and cabbage, adding the rosemary, thyme, sugar, salt, and pepper. Stir frequently, coating the vegetables in olive oil and herbs. Cook for about 10 minutes, until the onions begin to brown nicely.

When the cabbage is soft and the onions are caramelized, add the balsamic vinegar, vegetable broth, and bay leaf. Lower the heat and simmer slowly for one hour.

Lightly toast the slices of French bread. When the soup is ready, turn on your oven broiler. Ladle the soup into ovenproof bowls, and top with the French bread and a piece of cheese. Lightly broil the soup for about 3–4 minutes, until the cheese is starting to brown. Serve hot and bubbling.

Serves 4.

Winter Solstice Pumpkin Soup

Celebrate the Winter Solstice with this festive golden soup, warmed with fragrant nutmeg and allspice. This velvety soup is elegant and deceptively simple to prepare.

2 tablespoons extra-virgin olive oil

1 medium onion, diced

4 carrots, peeled, chopped

2 celery stalks, chopped

¼ teaspoon ground ginger

¼ teaspoon nutmeg

⅛ teaspoon allspice

½ teaspoon curry powder

Sea salt

White pepper, freshly ground

1 can (1 pound) pumpkin or 2 cups fresh, peeled, cubed

1 Yukon Gold (or yellow) potato, peeled, cubed

5 cups vegetable broth

2–3 tablespoons dry sherry

½ cup half-and-half or soy cream (optional)

In a heavy soup pot, heat the olive oil over medium heat and sauté the onion for about 5 minutes, until softened. Add in the chopped carrots and celery and stir in the spices. Lower the heat and gently cook for about 10 minutes, being careful not to overbrown the onions.

Add in the pumpkin, potato, and vegetable broth and stir. Add in the dry sherry, stir, and bring to a slow simmer, cooking the soup for about 25–35 minutes, until the vegetables are tender. Remove from heat.

Carefully ladle the soup into a blender. Cover and purée the soup until it is smooth and creamy. Return the purée to the soup pot and adjust the seasoning to your taste. Stir in the half-and-half, if desired, and blend till smooth. Serve at once in festive bowls with a basket of warm bread or muffins.

Serves 4–6.

Storm Moon Minestrone

On the night of the full moon, cook up a batch of this flavorful minestrone and serve it steaming hot, laying a stale bread slice into each bowl and drizzling extra-virgin olive oil all over the top.

3 tablespoons extra-virgin olive oil
1 medium red onion, diced
4 garlic cloves, minced
½ head white cabbage, cored, shredded thinly
4 carrots, peeled, coined
1 cup green beans, stemmed, cut into 2-inch lengths
1 zucchini, sliced, quartered
1 can (28 ounces) crushed Italian tomatoes
5 cups vegetable broth
1 cup white corn kernels, fresh or frozen
1 can (16 ounces) white northern (cannellini) beans, drained, rinsed
3 tablespoons fresh chopped Italian parsley
2 teaspoon dried basil
2 teaspoon marjoram
½ teaspoon thyme
1 bay leaf
  Sea salt
  Black pepper, freshly ground
1½ cups cooked spaghetti, cut into 3-inch pieces (optional)
  Parmesan cheese, shredded
  Garlic toast

In a heavy soup pot, heat the olive oil over medium heat and sauté the onion, until soft. Stir in the garlic, cabbage, carrots, green beans, and zucchini. Cook for 10 minutes. Add the tomatoes, vegetable broth, corn, cannellini beans, herbs, and seasonings. Gently simmer for 20 minutes. Add in cooked spaghetti pieces, if desired. Heat through for 5–10 more minutes.

Ladle into soup bowls and top with a spoonful of shredded Parmesan. Or lightly toast pieces of Italian or French bread, and rub them with a piece of fresh cut garlic. Lay a slice of the garlic toast on top of the minestrone and sprinkle with freshly grated Parmesan. Drizzle with extra-virgin olive oil, if desired.

Serves 4–6.

Hearty Chili Bean Soup

An easy, satisfying cold weather soup to warm you up on those frosty winter evenings. I put this recipe together on such a day, working with what I had on hand in my pantry. It was simply too cold for the Aphrodite in me to brave the bone-chilling temperature and venture out to the market!

2	tablespoons extra-virgin olive oil
5	garlic cloves, minced
½	teaspoon turmeric
½	teaspoon curry powder
½	teaspoon paprika
5	carrots, scrubbed, sliced
1	bunch scallions, sliced
1	can (28 ounces) crushed or chopped tomatoes
1–2	cups vegetable broth
2	cans (15 ounces each) chili or pinto beans, drained, rinsed
2	tablespoons dry sherry
1	bay leaf
	Sea salt
	Black pepper, freshly ground
2	cups torn dark salad greens (such as spinach, Swiss chard, escarole)
¼	cup chopped fresh parsley
	Light sour cream or yogurt

In a heavy soup pot, heat the olive oil over low-medium heat and gently cook the garlic and spices for 1 minute. Add in the carrots and scallions and sauté for 5 minutes. Add in the tomatoes, broth, beans, sherry, bay leaf, sea salt, and pepper. Bring to a high simmer.

Lower heat and gently simmer for 45 minutes to an hour. Add in the salad greens and parsley and continue to slow simmer for a minute or two, just until the greens are cooked. Remove the bay leaf and serve immediately.

Serve with warm cornbread and garnish with a swirl of light sour cream or yogurt.

Serves 4.

Winter Lentil Soup

The savory sweetness of carrots, cabbage, lentils, and curry in this aromatic soup might have even cheered Demeter in her season of sorrow.

2 tablespoons extra-virgin olive oil
1 medium onion, diced
1 leek, chopped, white part only
1 teaspoon cumin
1 teaspoon ginger
1 tablespoon curry powder
¼ teaspoon chili flakes
4 garlic cloves, minced
2 celery stalks, chopped
4 carrots, peeled, sliced
½ head white cabbage, cored, thinly shredded
1 can (28 ounces) plum tomatoes, with liquid
4 cups vegetable broth
½ cup dry sherry
1 cup lentils
Sea salt
White pepper, freshly ground
Yogurt or light sour cream
Fresh chives, chopped

In a heavy soup pot, heat the olive oil over medium heat and sauté the onion and leek for 3 minutes. Add in the spices and garlic, and sauté another minute or two. Add the celery, carrots, and cabbage. Stir and cook 5 minutes. Stir in the tomatoes, broth, sherry, lentils, salt, and pepper. Break apart the tomatoes a bit with a wooden spoon.

Cover and simmer on low for 35–45 minutes. Taste for seasoning adjustments, and periodically check lentils for tenderness. Continue simmering for 30 more minutes, or until the lentils are done.

Serve in colorful bowls and garnish with a swirl of yogurt or light sour cream and chopped chives.

Serves 4.

Serving ideas:
* Try topping with croutons and freshly shredded Parmesan.

Everyday Feasts

Polenta with Spinach and Portobello Mushrooms

I love the creamy texture of this country-style polenta, served up with garlicky portobello mushrooms and fresh spinach greens. For the shorter days of winter, this comforting dish warms the spirit with its down-to-earth simplicity.

4 cups vegetable broth
Sea salt
1½ cups stone-ground polenta cornmeal
2 cups milk
2–3 tablespoons extra-virgin olive oil
1 medium onion, sliced
3–5 garlic cloves, minced
2 portobello mushrooms, sliced
Balsamic vinegar
1 bunch fresh spinach, washed, stemmed
⅓ cup pine nuts
Asiago cheese, grated

In a heavy pot, bring the broth to a boil. Add a dash of sea salt. Begin to pour the cornmeal into the pot in a steady stream, stirring as you pour. (I like to use a whisk at this point to keep it from getting lumpy.) Lower the heat, pour in the milk, and continue stirring often, with a wooden spoon, as the polenta is cooking. The polenta is done when it begins to pull away from the side of the pan, about 20–25 minutes.

Heat the olive oil in a large skillet over low-medium heat. Lightly sauté the onion for 2–3 minutes, then add the garlic, mushrooms, and a dash of balsamic vinegar, until they begin to soften and brown slightly. Add the spinach and pine nuts, tossing the leaves to coat them in the garlicky oil. Cook briefly until the spinach is just wilted and remove from heat. Do not overcook.

Spoon the hot polenta immediately into warmed bowls and top with a spoonful of the mushrooms and spinach mixture. Sprinkle with grated Asiago.

Serves 4.

Roasted Vegetable Penne

The rich assortment of color and texture in this beautiful winter dish brings pleasure to both the eye and palate. Reds, soft yellows, deep oranges, and dark greens all dance on a bed of creamy white pasta. Serve at your table in a large pasta bowl for the admiring eyes of your family and friends.

1	large red onion, sliced into chunks
1	large red pepper, seeded, sliced into thin strips
2	portobello mushroom caps, sliced
2	cups broccoli florets
1	yellow squash, sliced into half moons
½	butternut squash, peeled, cubed
4	tablespoons extra-virgin olive oil
2–3	tablespoons balsamic vinegar
	Sea salt
	Black pepper, freshly ground
10	garlic cloves, peeled (sliced in half if the cloves are large)
1	teaspoon dried marjoram
¼	teaspoon fennel seed
1	pound Italian penne pasta
½	cup shredded Romano, Parmesan, or soy cheese

Preheat your oven to 400 degrees. Combine all of the vegetables in a large, oiled roasting pan and drizzle with the olive oil, balsamic vinegar, salt, pepper, garlic, marjoram, and fennel. Toss to coat evenly. Roast for about 30 minutes, or until vegetables are just tender, stirring occasionally so that the vegetables don't stick to the pan.

After the veggies have roasted for about 15 minutes, bring a large pot of salted water to a rolling boil and cook the penne until al dente. Warm up a large pasta serving bowl. When the pasta is ready, drain and toss with a drizzle of olive oil. Place the hot penne in the warmed pasta bowl, and toss with the shredded Parmesan cheese. Layer the roasted vegetables across the pasta in a generous display.

Serve at the table with more freshly grated cheese for garnish. A salad of mixed greens dressed in a *Balsamic Vinaigrette* (Winter, page 186) and a warm crusty loaf of bread complete the feast.

Serves 6.

Pasta with Spicy Peanut Sauce

Here is a sauce to awaken your senses and lift you out of the "Winter Doldrums." This flavorful peanutty sauce warms us up with its yang energy, and adds a touch of earth magick to any familiar pasta.

1 pound Italian pasta (linguini, spaghetti, or rotini)

2 tablespoons peanut oil or sesame oil

1 small red onion, minced

6 garlic cloves, minced

1 teaspoon curry powder

   Cayenne pepper

2 tablespoons tomato paste

⅔ cup natural peanut butter

1 teaspoon brown sugar

1 tablespoon soy sauce

3 tablespoons sherry vinegar

1½ cups hot vegetable broth

   Sea salt

   White pepper, freshly ground

4 green onions, chopped

   Flaked coconut

   Peanuts, chopped

Bring a large pot of fresh water to a rolling boil and cook the pasta to al dente. In a saucepan, heat the oil over medium heat and sauté the onion for about 5 minutes, until softened. Add the garlic, curry powder, and a good pinch or more of cayenne pepper and stir 1 minute. Mix in the tomato paste. Add the peanut butter, brown sugar, soy sauce, and vinegar, stirring to make a paste.

Slowly begin adding the hot vegetable broth, stirring well to blend. Heat through. Taste for seasoning adjustments and add salt and pepper to taste.

Drain the cooked pasta when ready, and pour it into a warmed serving bowl. Pour on the peanut sauce and toss well. Serve at the table, and offer small bowls of chopped green onions, flaked coconut, and chopped fresh peanuts for garnish.

Serves 4.

Serving idea

• This spicy peanutty sauce is also wonderful spooned over a slice of the *Scrumptious Nut Loaf* (Winter, page 174).

Linguini with White Vegetables and Pine Nuts

In honor of Brigid, a delectable recipe created in white on white. Snowy cauliflower and sweet cabbage are accented with the crunch of pine nuts on creamy white pasta. Wonderfully delicious.

1	pound Italian linguini
3	tablespoons extra-virgin olive oil
1	medium onion, diced
½	head cauliflower, cored, chopped into small pieces
½	head white cabbage, cored, thinly shredded
5–6	garlic cloves, minced
½	cup pine nuts
	Sea salt
	White pepper, freshly ground
¼	teaspoon fennel seed
	Juice of ½ lemon
3–4	tablespoons cream or soy cream
	Parmesan cheese, grated

Bring a large pot of fresh water to a rolling boil and cook the linguini till al dente. Warm up a large pasta serving bowl.

In a large skillet, heat the olive oil over medium heat and sauté the onion for 5 minutes, until soft. Add in the cauliflower, cabbage, garlic, pine nuts, sea salt, ground pepper, and fennel. Squeeze on the lemon juice. Sauté until the vegetables are tender and the pine nuts are toasted. Stir in the cream.

When the pasta is al dente, drain and pour the linguini into the warmed pasta bowl, and drizzle a little olive oil on the pasta to moisten it. Immediately add your white vegetables/pine nuts mixture and stir well.

Serve at the table with a small bowl of freshly grated Parmesan cheese for garnish.

Serves 4–5.

Winter Risotto with Mushrooms and Pine Nuts

The creaminess of this risotto, made with arborio rice, is complemented by the earthy mushrooms and crunchy pine nuts. This is pure comfort food any Goddess would savor on a blustery January day, while a fire crackles in the hearth.

2 tablespoons extra-virgin olive oil

1 medium onion, diced

5 garlic cloves, minced

1½ cups uncooked Italian arborio rice

2 cups chopped cremini or portobello mushrooms

½ cup red or white wine

4 cups hot vegetable broth

½ cup pine nuts, lightly toasted

2 tablespoons chopped fresh Italian parsley

1 teaspoon Italian herbs
Sea salt
White pepper, freshly ground

2 tablespoons soy cream or dairy cream (optional)
Parmesan cheese, grated
Fresh parsley, chopped

In a heavy saucepan, heat the olive oil over medium heat and sauté the onion and garlic for 3 minutes. Add the uncooked arborio rice and stir well to coat. Lightly sauté the rice until it is golden brown. Add the mushrooms and stir for 5 minutes. Add the wine and continue to stir until most of the wine is absorbed.

Add 1 cup of the hot broth and bring to a boil. Reduce heat and simmer, stirring frequently until most of the liquid is absorbed. Add the remaining broth 1 cup at a time, stirring and simmering the rice until each cup of broth is absorbed before adding the next one. (The whole process should take about 20 minutes or so.) Keep stirring and simmering until the liquid is absorbed and the rice is a creamy texture, yet still retains some "bite."

Stir in the toasted pine nuts, Italian herbs, and fresh chopped parsley. Season with sea salt and pepper, if desired. You may add in 2–3 tablespoons soy cream or dairy cream, if you like. Set aside for a few moments before serving.

Warm up four serving bowls. Spoon this creamy risotto into the warmed bowls, and garnish with a little freshly grated Parmesan and a sprinkling of chopped parsley.

Serves 4.

Black and White Enchiladas

Goddesses hardly ever see the world in black and white . . . unless perhaps you are an Athena. Here is a dish, then, that even an Athena would love.

2   tablespoons extra-virgin olive oil
1   onion, minced
4   garlic cloves, minced
2   teaspoons cumin
2   cans (1 pound each) black beans, drained, rinsed
1   can (1 pound) northern white (cannellini) beans, drained, rinsed
2   tablespoons chopped fresh cilantro
    Sea salt
    Black pepper, freshly ground
8   corn tortillas
2   cups *Simple Enchilada Sauce*
1   cup chopped green chilies
4   ounces feta cheese, crumbled, or a soy jack-style cheese, grated

Simple Enchilada Sauce
2   tablespoons extra-virgin olive oil
1   small onion, diced
4   garlic cloves, minced
1   teaspoon chili powder
1   teaspoon cumin
1   can (28 ounces) crushed tomatoes
1   teaspoon sugar
1   teaspoon sherry vinegar
2   teaspoons dried cilantro

Preheat your oven to 350 degrees. Heat the olive oil in a large skillet over medium heat and cook until the onion is softened, about 5 minutes. Add in the garlic and cumin and stir. Gently cook for 1 minute and remove from heat.

Combine the beans gently in a mixing bowl. Stir in the cilantro and season with sea salt and freshly ground pepper. Pour the onion mixture over the beans and gently mix.

Oil a clay or ceramic shallow baking dish. Lay a tortilla flat, and spoon ⅛ of the bean filling across the center of the tortilla. Roll it up, placing it into the baking dish, seam-side down. Repeat with the other tortillas, fitting them snugly against each other. Top with *Simple Enchilada Sauce* (below), green chilies (hot or mild), and crumbled feta or soy cheese. Bake for 25–35 minutes, until hot and bubbling.

Serve the enchiladas with *Spanish Rice* (Autumn, page 135) and a crisp salad of mixed greens. Offer your favorite salsa and a garnish of light sour cream, if desired.

Serves 4.

Simple Enchilada Sauce

Heat the oil in a saucepan over medium heat and sauté the onion, garlic, and spices for 5 minutes. Add the tomatoes, sugar, vinegar, and cilantro and bring to a simmer. Cover and cook 15 minutes. Use as a sauce for enchiladas, burritos, or casseroles.

Stuffed Cabbage in Marinara Sauce

The stuffed cabbage I remember as a child was filled with ground beef and onions. Here is my Vegetarian Goddess version, with fragrant Mediterranean seasonings.

1 large head white
 cabbage
1 tablespoon extra-
 virgin olive oil
1 onion, diced
5 garlic cloves, minced
1 cup chopped
 portobello or
 cremini mushrooms
2½ cups cooked Texmati
 rice
1 free-range egg or egg
 substitute
½ cup pine nuts
3 tablespoons chopped
 fresh Italian parsley
2 tablespoons chopped
 fresh mint
1 teaspoon marjoram
½ teaspoon cumin
 Sea salt
 Black pepper, freshly
 ground
2–3 cups *Basic Fresh
 Marinara Sauce*

Preheat your oven to 325 degrees. Core the head of a cabbage and boil until the leaves are tender. Drain and separate the leaves and set them aside.

In a medium skillet, heat the olive oil and gently cook the onion and garlic for 5 minutes. Add in the chopped mushrooms and cook for 5 more minutes, until softened. Remove from heat and set aside.

In a large mixing bowl, combine the cooked rice, onion/mushroom mixture, egg, pine nuts, herbs, and spices. Spoon a heaping tablespoonful of this rice mixture onto the thicker end of the cabbage leaf and fold over, folding the edges in toward the center, rolling up snugly. Place in an oiled baking dish. Repeat until the filling is gone.

Cover the stuffed cabbage with the *Basic Fresh Marinara Sauce* (Autumn, page 119) and bake for 1½ hours. Serve this warming dish along with a bowl of soup and some hot, fresh rolls or corn muffins.

Serves 4–6.

Red, White, and Green Lasagna

This version of lasagna features silken tofu, dark green spinach, and creamy white cauliflower in a red tomato sauce. Although it takes some time to assemble, it is perfect for making ahead.

9–10 lasagna noodles

1 pound firm silken tofu

2 free-range eggs or egg substitute

¾ cup freshly shredded Parmesan or soy cheese

Sea salt

White pepper, freshly ground

¼ cup chopped fresh Italian parsley

1 teaspoon marjoram

1 teaspoon Italian herbs

¼ cup pine nuts

1 tablespoon extra-virgin olive oil

1 onion, diced

½ head of cauliflower, cored, chopped into small pieces

6 garlic cloves, crushed

1 bunch fresh spinach, washed, stemmed

4 cups *Basic Fresh Marinara Sauce*

5 roma tomatoes, sliced

¼ cup freshly shredded Parmesan or soy cheese

Rosemary sprigs

Preheat your oven to 350 degrees. Prepare lasagna noodles according to package directions and drain. Drizzle or spray with olive oil to keep them from sticking and lay flat.

In a mixing bowl, mash the tofu with the eggs, Parmesan, salt, pepper, and herbs. Add in the pine nuts and blend. Set aside.

In a large skillet, heat the olive oil over medium heat and sauté the onion for 5 minutes, until softened. Add in the cauliflower and garlic. Stir and cook until the cauliflower is tender. Pour onto a plate and return the skillet to the burner. Cover the bottom of the pan with a scant amount of water and bring to a boil. Toss in the spinach leaves and steam for 3–4 minutes, until wilted. Drain and lay on paper towels.

Lightly oil a 9 by 13-inch baking dish and spoon in enough marinara sauce to cover the bottom. Lay three of the noodles on the bottom of the pan. Top with ½ of the tofu mixture, then ½ of the cauliflower mixture, and ½ of the wilted spinach leaves. Cover with ⅓ of the *Basic Fresh Marinara Sauce* (Autumn, page 119). Place another layer of noodles, tofu mixture, cauliflower mixture, and the spinach and top with ⅓ of the sauce. Cover with a final layer of noodles and sauce. Arrange sliced tomatoes all over the top and dust with Parmesan and herbs.

Bake for 35 minutes, or until hot and bubbly. Let the lasagna stand for 10 minutes before slicing and serving. Garnish with fresh rosemary sprigs.

Serves 6–8.

Baked Spaghetti Squash

I have always loved this quirky vegetable, a squash that cooks up like spaghetti. Who says Mother Nature doesn't have a sense of humor?

1 medium-large spaghetti squash

Sea salt

Black pepper, freshly ground

3–4 tablespoons extra-virgin olive oil

4 garlic cloves, minced

1 cup roma tomatoes, chopped

1 teaspoon lemon juice

3 tablespoons chopped fresh Italian parsley

1 tablespoon chopped fresh basil

1 teaspoon marjoram

6 ounces feta cheese or goat cheese

Fresh parsley, chopped

Preheat your oven to 350 degrees. Cut the squash in half, lengthwise, and remove the seeds. Season with sea salt and ground pepper. Place the squash in a roasting pan, cut side down. Pour about an inch of water into the bottom of the pan to keep the squash from scorching. Bake for 40–45 minutes, until fork-tender.

In a skillet, heat the olive oil and garlic over low-medium heat for 3 minutes. Add in the tomatoes, lemon juice, herbs, and more salt and pepper. Heat through, gently simmering for about 10 minutes.

When the squash is done, remove it from the oven. Carefully lift it out of the pan and set it on a cutting board. Using a fork, scrape the inside of the squash to pull out the long spaghetti-like strands, placing them in a warm serving dish.

Drizzle the squash strands with a little extra-virgin olive oil and toss gently. Spoon on the hot tomato-garlic mixture, using a fork to work some of the sauce down into the squash. Crumble the feta over the top (or dot with dabs of goat cheese), and add some fresh chopped parsley for garnish.

Serve in warmed pasta bowls with *Rosemary Focaccia* (Summer, pages 56–57) and a glass of your favorite Italian wine.

Serves 4.

Scrumptious Nut Loaf

This flavorful Vegetarian Goddess version features the crunch of ground nuts and the earthiness of mushrooms, grounding earth energy with moon magick. Scrumptious!

1½   cups mixed nuts
     (pecans, cashews, wal-
     nuts, almonds, peanuts)
2   tablespoons extra-virgin
     olive oil
½   large yellow onion, diced
4   garlic cloves, minced
½   cup chopped cremini
     mushrooms
1   cup Italian seasoned
     bread crumbs
¾–1 cup plain soy or almond
     milk
1   free-range egg, beaten,
     or egg substitute
1   tablespoon Worcestershire
     sauce
1   carrot, peeled, grated
½   cup chopped water
     chestnuts
1   tablespoon chopped
     fresh parsley
1   teaspoon Italian herbs
1   teaspoon curry powder
     Nutmeg
     Sea salt
     Black pepper, freshly
     ground
¾   cup good, chunky
     tomato sauce
3   tablespoons yogurt or
     light sour cream
     Cinnamon

Process or finely chop the mixed nuts. Heat the olive oil in a skillet over medium heat and sauté the onion and garlic for 3–4 minutes. Add in the mushrooms and sauté for another 3 minutes, until tender.

In a large bowl, combine the ground nuts with the onion/mushroom mixture. Add in the bread crumbs, soy milk, egg, Worcestershire sauce, carrots, water chestnuts, parsley, herbs, curry, nutmeg, sea salt, and black pepper. Mix well and allow to stand for 10 minutes.

Preheat your oven to 350 degrees. Spoon the mixture into an oiled loaf pan and press firmly. Cover with foil and bake for 25 minutes. Uncover and increase oven temperature to 400 degrees. Bake 20–25 minutes until golden brown. Let it sit for 10 minutes before you slice and serve it.

To make the sauce, in a small saucepan, combine the tomato sauce with yogurt or sour cream, and blend well. Add a dash of cinnamon. Heat through gently.

Slice the loaf and serve on warmed plates. Spoon the sauce over each slice of the nut loaf for a perfect accompaniment.

Serves 4–6.

Potato Lover's Pizza

One of the first conversations I remember having with my husband, at a painting workshop years ago, was about putting potatoes on a pizza. It warmed my Celtic heart!

2 tablespoons extra-virgin olive oil

1 red onion, sliced

8 garlic cloves, sliced

4–6 small red potatoes, scrubbed, sliced thinly

2–3 tablespoons water

3 tablespoons pine nuts

1 bunch fresh spinach, washed, stemmed

Pizza Dough, stretched and rolled out

½ cup *Sun-Dried Tomato Basil Pesto* or favorite pesto

1 teaspoon Italian herbs

1 teaspoon marjoram

4 ounces feta cheese, crumbled

Preheat your oven to 400 degrees. In a large skillet, heat the olive oil over medium high and sauté the onion for 5 minutes. Add in the garlic slices and potatoes and stir for 3 minutes. Add 2–3 tablespoons water, cover, and cook until tender, about 6 minutes. Add pine nuts and stir. Add in the spinach leaves and cook until just wilted. Remove from heat.

Spread the *Sun-Dried Tomato Basil Pesto* (Summer, page 58) on the prepared *Pizza Dough* (page 26). Lay the onions, potatoes, garlic, pine nuts, and spinach leaves evenly over the pesto and sprinkle with herbs. Crumble feta cheese over the pizza and drizzle a little olive oil over the potatoes and around the outer crust edges.

Bake for 15–20 minutes until the pizza dough is baked to a golden brown. Serve with a light green salad and a glass of good chianti.

Serves 3–4.

Mushroom Marinara Calzone

Warm, fresh bread dough wrapped around sautéed mushrooms in a fragrant marinara sauce, with melted provolone . . . what more could you ask for? Those Italian Goddesses sure know how to make a sandwich.

1 tablespoon extra-virgin olive oil

½ onion, diced

8 ounces sliced cremini mushrooms

1 teaspoon Italian herbs Calzone bread dough, prepared, risen

3–4 tablespoons *Basic Fresh Marinara Sauce*

4 ounces sliced Italian provolone or provolone-style soy cheese

In a medium skillet, heat the olive oil over medium heat and sauté the onion for 3 minutes. Add the mushrooms and herbs, cooking until soft. Set aside.

Preheat your oven to 350 degrees. For the calzone bread dough, follow the directions for preparing and rising in the *Spinach and Feta Calzone* recipe (Spring, page 24).

Take the risen dough and punch it down. Roll it out to a 10 to 14-inch square. Spoon the mushrooms down the center of the dough. Add the *Basic Fresh Marinara Sauce* (Autumn, page 119) and top with provolone slices.

Fold over one side of the dough to cover the filling, and repeat with the opposite side, folding it over like a blanket. Turn in and pinch the ends to seal.

Place on an oiled baking sheet and bake for 20–30 minutes, until a nice golden brown. Let it cool to room temperature and cut the calzone into 2-inch servings.

Serves 4.

Note your own favorite calzone stuffings:

Nancy's Vegetarian Hoppin' John

To celebrate the traditional coming New Year, cooks in the American South simmer up batches of spicy black-eyed peas and rice, believing that the custom of eating Hoppin' John on New Year's Day will bring luck and prosperity to the household. This recipe is an adapted version from my friend Nancy . . . a powerful Bicycle-Riding Goddess.

1	pound dried black-eyed peas
1	bay leaf
1	teaspoon oregano
½	teaspoon thyme
1	teaspoon dried cilantro or basil
	Cayenne pepper
	Sea salt
	Black pepper, freshly ground
2	tablespoons extra-virgin olive oil
2	red onions, chopped
1	yellow pepper, cored, seeded, chopped
2	celery stalks, chopped
4–5	garlic cloves, minced
1	can (28 ounces) tomatoes
2½	cups cooked brown rice
	Red onion, chopped

Rinse and clean the black-eyed peas, then soak them in fresh cold water overnight. Drain and rinse the beans, pouring them into a heavy soup pot and covering them with more fresh cold water. Bring to a boil and add in the bay leaf, oregano, thyme, cilantro, cayenne, sea salt, and black pepper. Lower the heat, cover, and simmer for 2–3 hours, checking every so often, adding more water if necessary.

In a medium skillet, heat the olive oil and sauté the onion for 3 minutes. Add in the chopped yellow pepper, celery, and garlic and sauté until tender.

When the black-eyed peas are done, add the sautéed vegetables, tomatoes, and cooked brown rice. Stir together well and heat through for another 5–10 minutes. Taste and make seasoning adjustments.

Serve in large pottery soup plates, garnish with chopped red onion, and pass the Cajun hot sauce! (Don't forget the cornbread.)

Serves 4–6.

Savory Sides

Dijon Roasted Onions and Potatoes

The unbeatable combination of potato and onion is roasted with Dijon mustard and savory herbs for a grounding, warming side dish.

4 large Yukon Gold potatoes, scrubbed, cut into wedges
2 onions, thickly sliced
3 tablespoons extra-virgin olive oil
5 garlic cloves, minced
½ cup good Dijon mustard
½ teaspoon marjoram
½ teaspoon rosemary
Curry powder
Sea salt
Black pepper, freshly ground

Preheat your oven to 400 degrees. In a large bowl, combine the potatoes and onions with olive oil, garlic, mustard, herbs, and seasonings. Stir until well coated.

Pour the potato mixture into a clay or glass baking dish, or an oiled roasting pan. Roast for 25–35 minutes, until potatoes are fork-tender.

Serves 4–6.

Maple-Baked Acorn Squash

It is evident throughout this book how much I love roasted vegetables. Roasting coaxes forth a natural sweetness and flavor that all Goddesses love.

2 acorn squash, halved, seeded
Sea salt
2 tablespoons extra-virgin olive oil
2 tablespoons real maple syrup
⅛ teaspoon cinnamon
⅛ teaspoon allspice

Preheat your oven to 350 degrees. Place squash halves, cut side up, in an oiled roasting pan. Sprinkle with salt and pour an inch or so of water into the pan (to keep the bottoms from scorching).

In a glass measuring cup, combine the olive oil, maple syrup, and spices, stirring to mix well. Pour this sweet syrup all around the cut edges of the squash, letting it drizzle down into the center.

Bake for 35–45 minutes, until the squash is fork-tender. Remove carefully. Serve on a warm plate as is, or cut the squash into wedges, drizzling the pieces with any escaped syrup.

Serves 4.

Roasted Winter Vegetables

My favorite way to celebrate the variety of vegetables the Goddess provides for us is to combine every vegetable I can think of, toss them together in olive oil, and roast them to sweet perfection. One example follows . . . create your own favorite combinations.

1   small winter squash (butternut, acorn, etc.), peeled, seeded, cut into chunks
1   onion, peeled, thickly sliced
2   carrots, peeled, diagonally sliced
2   red or gold potatoes, scrubbed, cut into wedges
1   medium sweet potato or yam, peeled, cut into wedges
1   small head broccoli, cut into florets
1   sweet pepper, any color, seeded, cut into chunks
8   garlic cloves, peeled
4   tablespoons extra-virgin olive oil
½   teaspoon rosemary
    Thyme
    Sea salt
    Black pepper, freshly ground

Preheat your oven to 350 degrees. In an oiled roasting pan or large clay baking dish, combine the cut vegetables and toss with the olive oil and herbs. Season with sea salt and black pepper. Roast for 45–55 minutes, until the vegetables are fork-tender and slightly browned.

Note: If you prefer vegetables that are less crispy and more moist, choose a covered clay dish to roast them in. The vegetables become sweet and tender, with a subtle infusion of the seasonings.

Serves 4–6.

Roasted Ginger Sweet Potatoes

A nutty, gingery confection of sweet potatoes that will enhance any of your favorite cold weather foods.

1   pound sweet potatoes, peeled, cubed

2–3   tablespoons extra-virgin olive oil

½   cup honey or real maple syrup

1–2   teaspoons grated ginger

1   teaspoon Chinese five-spice powder or ½ teaspoon cinnamon

     Black pepper, freshly ground

½   cup chopped pecans or walnuts

Preheat your oven to 375 degrees. Combine potatoes, olive oil, honey, and spices, tossing well. Lightly oil a medium-sized baking dish and spoon in the potato mixture. Top with chopped pecans or walnuts.

Bake for 35–40 minutes. Cover with foil halfway through baking if the nuts are getting too brown.

Serves 4.

Cranberry Walnut Pilaf

A festive variation on the classic rice pilaf, the tartness of cranberries and warmth of toasted walnuts make this a perfect winter side dish.

¼ cup walnuts, chopped

2 tablespoons extra-virgin olive oil

1 medium red onion, diced

1 cup short grain brown rice, uncooked

2½ cups hot vegetable broth

2 tablespoons dry sherry

½ cup dried cranberries

Gently heat a spray of olive oil in a nonstick saucepan and lightly toast the chopped walnuts for about 3–4 minutes. Remove the walnuts to a small dish and return the pan to the burner. Now add the olive oil to your pan and sauté the onion for 5 minutes. Add in the uncooked rice and lightly stir-fry for 4–5 minutes, until the rice begins to turn golden brown.

Add in the hot vegetable broth and sherry, and bring to a boil. Cover and reduce the heat to low. Simmer until all the liquid is absorbed, about 45 minutes. Stir in the cranberries and toasted walnuts, mixing well. Cover and heat through for 5 minutes.

Serves 4.

Serving idea

- Try this pilaf as a side dish for *Scrumptious Nut Loaf* (Winter, page 174) or pair it with *Roasted Winter Vegetables* (Winter, page 181).

Winter Salads

Winter Greens

A crisp, chilled salad may not be an inviting choice on a gray, frigid day, but that doesn't mean that we have to give up on our fresh greens during the cold winter months. Try warming and grounding greens by wilting them in a skillet with fruity olive oil and garlic.

2–3　tablespoons extra-virgin olive oil

2–3　garlic cloves, minced or crushed

1½　cups fresh greens per person (include baby spinach, Swiss chard, arugula, endive, or escarole)

Dijon Vinaigrette

4　tablespoons extra-virgin olive oil

2　tablespoons white wine vinegar

2　heaping teaspoons Dijon mustard

1　teaspoon dill

¼　teaspoon sea salt

¼　teaspoon freshly ground black pepper

Heat the olive oil gently in a large skillet and toss in the garlic. Cook the garlic lightly, for 2–3 minutes. After the greens are washed, toss them, still damp, into the warm garlicky olive oil and briefly turn them just until they begin to wilt. Serve the greens as is, in the warmed oil and garlic.

Or, if you prefer, lightly heat the greens in a skillet with a little water instead, and then dress them in a room-temperature vinaigrette, such as the *Dijon Vinaigrette* that follows.

Dijon Vinaigrette

Goddesses love this easy vinaigrette spiked with the flavors of Dijon and dill.

Whisk together all of the ingredients and pour over salad greens.

Chilled Winter Greens in Balsamic Vinaigrette

Choose an assortment of your favorite greens, such as spinach and chicory, and dress in the balsamic vinaigrette.

4 tablespoons extra-virgin olive oil
4 tablespoons balsamic vinegar
2 teaspoons Italian herbs
Sea salt
Salad greens, chilled

Whisk together the ingredients and pour over the chilled salad greens.

Serving idea

- This vinaigrette is also wonderful drizzled on grilled or roasted vegetables.

Sweet Endings

Midwinter Gingerbread

A Yuletide classic, this spicy-sweet bread is also wonderful sliced, toasted, and buttered for an afternoon tea, accompanied by a warm, cozy throw and a good book.

½ stick butter or solid margarine

½ cup molasses

1 large free-range egg

½ cup brown sugar

1 cup unbleached all-purpose flour

2 teaspoons cinnamon

2 teaspoons ginger

¼ teaspoon cloves

¼ teaspoon salt

1 teaspoon baking soda

½ cup boiling water

½ cup orange marmalade or good apricot jam

½ cup finely chopped pecans or walnuts (optional)

Preheat oven to 350 degrees. In a small saucepan, gently melt the butter with the molasses and set aside. In a mixing bowl, combine the egg and brown sugar and beat well. Pour in the melted butter/molasses mixture and beat with an electric mixer to blend well. Then, by hand, stir in the flour, spices, and salt, just enough to blend.

Add the baking soda to the boiling water and stir well. Pour this soda water into the batter and gently mix. Add the marmalade and pecans, again, stirring just until mixed in.

Pour the gingerbread batter into a lightly greased 8 by 8-inch or 9 by 9-inch pan. Bake for about 30 minutes. The gingerbread is ready when a toothpick inserted into the center emerges clean. Let the pan cool for 10 minutes, then insert a knife around the edges of the pan to loosen the bread. Gently invert, placing it onto a plate.

Serve simply as squares dusted with powdered sugar or topped with a spoonful of fresh whipped cream.

Serves 8.

Tiramisu

Originating in Italy, this heavenly dessert is a divine midwinter treat. Just when we need it most—a snowy white melt-in-your-mouth indulgence.

12 small dessert-size
    sponge cakes
1 cup whipping cream
3 tablespoons sugar
4 ounces pasteurized
    egg whites
½ cup sugar
15 ounces whole-milk
    ricotta cheese
1 teaspoon bourbon
    vanilla
1 cup cold strong coffee
¼ cup Kahlua
    Unsweetened cocoa
    Quick Chocolate
    Sauce

Set the sponge cakes on a cookie sheet and medium broil them for about 1 minute, just enough to gently toast them. Set aside to cool.

In a small mixing bowl, whip the cream with 3 tablespoons sugar, until it forms stiff peaks. Set aside. In a medium bowl, whip the egg whites and sugar until stiff. Gently fold in the ricotta and vanilla, then gently fold in the whipped cream, taking care not to overblend. Set aside.

To prepare the sponge cakes, stir the Kahlua into the cold strong coffee. In a medium-sized oval dish or casserole, place 6 of the cooled sponge cakes in the bottom, squeezing them in tightly to fit. Brush them generously with half of the coffee mixture. Then slather on half of the whipped cream mixture. Top with a second layer of the sponge cakes. Brush the cakes with the remaining coffee and top with the remainder of the whipped cream mixture. Cover and refrigerate a minimum of 4–6 hours; overnight is even better.

When you are ready to serve, make the *Quick Chocolate Sauce* (page 189). Plate the Tiramisu by first drizzling a little chocolate sauce around the serving plate. Using a spatula, cut and slice a piece of the Tiramisu. It will be a bit messy, but don't worry. Once on the plate, drizzle more chocolate sauce in a spiral over the top. Lightly dust the whole plate with a whisper of cocoa . . . and serve with a knowing smile.

Serves 6–8, depending upon appetites!

continued

Quick Chocolate Sauce

Pour the condensed milk into a small heavy saucepan (use a double boiler if you have one, or even microwaving in a glass cup works). Slowly heat the milk on low, until it starts to bubble.

Remove from heat and stir in the semi-sweet chocolate until it melts. Stir in the Kahlua and test the consistency. The sauce should run freely. Add more Kahlua to thin it, if you need to.

Quick Chocolate Sauce

½ cup sweetened condensed milk

4 ounces Ghirardelli or Toblerone semi-sweet chocolate (chips or bar)

2 tablespoons Kahlua

Hazelnut Ice Cream

Creamy and cold as winter snow, with the inviting crunch of hazelnuts from the hazel tree of the Goddess Artemis. You may make this confection with or without dairy . . . both ways are delicious.

½ cup half-and-half or nondairy cream

1½ cups milk or almond milk

1 cup sugar or ½ cup honey

½ cup pasteurized egg substitute

1 teaspoon bourbon vanilla extract

1½ teaspoons hazelnut extract (optional)

1 teaspoon xanthan gum

¼ cup chopped hazelnuts

Combine the half-and-half, milk, sugar, egg substitute, flavor extracts, and xanthan gum in a blender. Cover and purée for 3 minutes, until frothy and creamy. Pour into the container of your ice cream maker and stir in the hazelnuts. Freeze according to the manufacturer's instructions.

Note: I use a pasteurized egg substitute such as Egg Beaters in my frozen dessert recipes, not only because they are fat and cholesterol-free, but safer as well. Raw eggs may contain harmful bacteria. I do not ever recommend using unpastuerized raw eggs in an ice cream recipe.

Serves 4–5.

Pear Crisp

Delight your family and guests with this yummy, old-fashioned baked dessert, spiced with cinnamon for luck and love!

4	large ripe Bartlett pears, washed, peeled, sliced
⅓	cup dried cranberries
⅓	cup apple or pear juice
¼	cup brown sugar, packed
1	teaspoon cinnamon
	Nutmeg
1	cup light granola
4	tablespoons stick margarine

Preheat oven to 350 degrees. Lightly grease a glass pie dish (8 or 9-inch) with margarine. Arrange the pear slices around the dish, overlapping as you go. Sprinkle on the cranberries and drizzle on the fruit juice.

In a separate bowl, combine the brown sugar, cinnamon, and a pinch of nutmeg with the granola, and mix well. Layer this topping evenly over the sliced pears. Dot with pieces of margarine.

Bake for 50 minutes, until the juices are bubbling. Serve warm or refrigerate for later. (To reheat, cover with foil and place in a 325-degree oven just until warm.)

Notes on your favorite
Winter recipes

Index

Food Category List

If there is more than one page number attributed to a recipe, the actual page number of the recipe is in bold type.

Alphabetical List

If there is more than one page number attributed to a recipe, the actual page number of the recipe is in bold type.